# Insights into New Creation

*For Parents and Teachers Using
The New Creation Series*

Richard Reichert

Religious Education Division
Wm. C. Brown Company Publishers
Dubuque, Iowa

Nihil Obstat
    Rev. Richard Schaefer

Imprimatur
    ✝Most Rev. Daniel W. Kucera, O.S.B.
    Archbishop of Dubuque

October 29, 1984

The Nihil Obstat and the Imprimatur are official declarations that a book or a pamphlet is free of doctrinal or moral error. No implication is contained therein that those who have granted the Nihil Obstat or Imprimatur agree with the contents, opinions, or statements expressed.

**Program Consultants**

Theological Consultant—Rev. John Forliti, Director of Youth Programs, Search Institute, Minneapolis, Minnesota; author of *Reverence for Life and Family Program*.

Pedagogical Consultant—Sister John Martin Sullivan, A.S.C.J.

Medical Consultant—Mark J. Popp, M.D.

Excerpts from EDUCATION IN HUMAN SEXUALITY FOR CHRISTIANS, copyright © 1981, by the Publications Office, United States Catholic Conference, Department of Education, Washington, D.C., are used by permission of copyright owner. All rights reserved.

No part of this book may be reprinted or transmitted in any form or by any means, electronic or mechanical, or by any information retrieval system without permission in writing from the publisher.

Copyright © 1985 Wm. C. Brown Company Publishers.
Manufactured in the United States of America.
All rights reserved.

ISBN 0-697-02000-2

10   9   8   7   6   5   4   3

# Contents

NEW CREATION: Catechesis in Human Sexuality ........... v
Introduction ................................................................. 1

1   Who Is Responsible for Sexuality Education ............. 3
2   What Are the Goals of Sexuality Education? ............ 9
3   When to Teach What .............................................. 23
4   How to Approach Sexuality Education .................... 41

Appendix I ................................................................. 57
Appendix II ............................................................... 65
Appendix III .............................................................. 77
Bibliography ............................................................. 83

# NEW CREATION: Catechesis in Human Sexuality

## Introducing NEW CREATION

Since Vatican II an increasing number of mandates have come forth from the Church's teaching authority regarding the need for providing children and young people with "positive and prudent sex education " (Declaration on Education, Vatican Council II, no. 1). The United States Conference of Catholic Bishops in numerous pastoral letters has affirmed "the value and necessity of wisely planned education of children in human sexuality," as has the National Catechetical Directory, *Sharing the Light of Faith.* Most recently, the need was affirmed by the Sacred Congregation for Catholic Education in Rome (Educational Guidance in Human Love).

In all its documents, of course, the Church has always recognized that the primary responsibility for education in sexuality belongs to parents within their families. However, the Church also, just as seriously, recognizes its own responsibility in supporting, supplementing, and carrying forward education in sexuality through its schools and educational programs. NEW CREATION, a program of catechesis in human sexuality, is designed to aid both parents and teachers in their task. It is a guided, consistent, holistic, and faith-filled approach to catechesis in human sexuality. The series is rooted in the belief that in and through Jesus humankind has indeed become a new creation, totally acceptable to the Father. The ultimate goal of the NEW CREATION series is to provide children with an understanding of the nature and importance of human sexuality as informed by Christian faith.

Most parents and teachers have some very important questions that need to be addressed regarding catechesis in human sexuality particularly regarding this series. Among these questions are the following:

What assumptions underlie the NEW CREATION program?

- Within the Christian community, there is a need for giving *gradual* and *positive* sexual education to children. (Educational Guidance in Human Love, no. 106)
- The prime responsibility for education in human sexuality belongs to parents. The family is the first school and the best place for securing a "gradual education in human love." (Educational Guidance in Human Love, no. 48)
- Providing education in human sexuality, in collaboration with parents, is a responsibility shared by other persons and institutions within the Christian community, specifically the school and the parish. (Educational Guidance in Human Love, no. 54)
- A formal program of catechesis in human sexuality should serve as an aid to parents; it should reinforce and support parents in their task; it should supplement and complete their task. (Educational Guidance in Human Love, no. 59 and no. 69)
- Human sexuality education must never be reduced to biology but must always be associated with Christian values and moral principles. (Educational Guidance in Human Love, no. 19)

Why is there a need for a formal program of catechesis in human sexuality if sexual education is the primary responsibility of parents?

- Because parents want and need assistance.

    A poll conducted by the Gallup Researchers in 1977 established that a broad base of support exists for education in human sexuality. The report showed that 77 percent of their respondents favored sexual education in the schools. Moreover, the poll noted that Catholics showed no major differences with the rest of the respondents in their support of education in human sexuality. Educational Guidance in Human Love also spoke to the need parents have for assistance in their task of sexual education.

- Because some parents do not fulfill their responsibilities and the child should not be allowed to suffer for the parent's failure.

The National Catechetical Directory pointed out that parents need assistance in catechizing their children on the subject of sexuality. A footnote included in the National Catechetical Directory reported that it was found in one study, that only 12 percent of young people are taught about sex by their parents. Most learn from their peers. (See: *Adolescent Appraisals and Selected Institutions* [home, church, school, youth organizations], Calderwood, Deryck. Oregon State University, 1970.)

- Because the Church teaches that human sexual education is an important priority in Christian education which can be met in part through approved programs. (To Teach as Jesus Did, no. 56 and Educational Guidance in Human Love, no. 17)
- Because children need to experience a community beyond the family which also holds Christian values, in order to counteract the negative attitudes and values being portrayed by the media. (Pope John Paul II to members of the Pontifical Council for the Family, August, 1984)

What is the purpose of a program of formal instruction in human sexuality?

- To help parents fulfill their obligation to provide such education. (To Teach as Jesus Did, no. 57)
- To protect young people from the dangers of ignorance and widespread degradation. (Educational Guidance in Human Love, no. 12)
- To support, supplement, and carry forward education in human sexuality. (Educational Guidance in Human Love, no. 54)

Why does the NEW CREATION program include topics of a specifically sexual nature in all books from grade one through grade eight?

- Because it is specifically a program of catechesis in human sexuality, and according to Church teaching (contained in a variety of documents), catechesis in human sexuality is to be provided not simply around the time of puberty, but throughout the growing years, from infancy to adulthood. The National Catechetical Directory, for example, states that "education in sexuality includes all dimensions of the topic: moral, spiritual, psychological, emotional, and physical" . . . and that "education which helps people understand and accept their sexuality begins in infancy and continues at adulthood." (National Catechetical Directory, no. 191)

- Because the child's needs require it. (*To Teach as Jesus Did,* no. 58; Educational Guidance in Human Love, no. 42)
- Because the Church teaches that sexuality education should be provided gradually and progressively rather than abruptly or all at once. (Human Life in Our Day, no. 63; Educational Guidance in Human Love, no. 48)
- Because the psychology of the child requires that information be provided gradually.

Msgr. George A. Kelly in *Your Child and Sex, A Guide for Catholic Parents* advises parents to "Make the education gradual rather than abrupt" (page 26). Msgr. Kelly notes that many young children raise questions early regarding sex and sexuality. He also points out that "a parent who displays a desire to be helpful and a willingness to be frank will be of greater service to a child than one who has the technical information but does not wish to discuss the subject truthfully."

- Because children raise questions of a specifically sexual nature, often as soon as they are able to talk, and it is important that these questions be answered so that an attitude of openness and positive acceptance is nurtured in the child. (See Very Reverend Monsignor George A. Kelly in *Your Child and Sex, A Guide for Catholic Parents.* New York: Random House, 1964; Arnold Gesell M.D., and Francis Ilg, M.D., and Louise Bates Ames, Ph.D. in *The Child from Five to Ten.* New York: Harper & Row Publishers, 1977; Esther D. Schulz, Ph.D., and Sally R. Williams, R.N. in *Family Life and Sex Education: Curriculum and Instruction.* New York: Harcourt, Brace and World, Inc., 1969.)

What sexual questions do young children have?

Research tells us that the common questions of young children, ages three to four, are:

What are these (genitals) called?
Why doesn't a girl have a penis?
Why is daddy's penis bigger?
Where do babies come from?
How does the baby get inside the mother?
Where does a baby come out?
Does having a baby hurt?
Why can't men have babies?
Why do grown-up women have breasts?
Will I have a baby?

The questions of five- to eight-year-olds often include the following, according to research:

How do the mother's egg and father's sperm get together?

Is (semen) the same as (urine)?

Why doesn't the mother's egg go into the father?

How does a baby eat and breath inside a mother?

Why do I have a belly button?

Why does a mother get so big when she is having a baby?

How big is a baby inside a mother?

Note: For more information regarding the questions children typically have regarding sex and sexuality, see the sources referred to in the previous questions and also, *What to Tell Your Children about Sex* published by the Child Study Association of America and *When Children Ask about Sex*, a guide for parents by Joae Graham Selzer, M.D., child psychologist and faculty member, Harvard Medical School.

Is it really necessary that the questions children have about sex be answered?

- Most researchers are in agreement that the answer is YES, children's questions ought to be answered honestly and frankly. As the Church says, "Progressive information requires a partial explanation, but always according to truth. Explanations must not be distorted by reticence or by lack of frankness." (Educational Guidance in Human Love, no. 87) As Monsignor George Kelly notes, "Children form impressions from the way adults respond to questions asked." Suppose a child asks, "How does the father's penis get into the mother's body?" His mother answers curtly, "In a special way. Now run upstairs this moment and wash your hands or read a book, or play with your toys." He will get the message: This is a subject his mother wants to get rid of as quickly as possible. If she answers simply that God has made a place for the penis in mother's body, the chances are that he will be satisfied and—up to the limit of his ability—somewhat informed." Monsignor Kelly cautions, "Our reactions to words depend entirely upon our training: we react as we have been taught to react. If you give your child the impression that words which accurately describe the sexual organs are indecent, he may have a difficult time ever using these words, even as an adult, without embarrassment. For this reason, you should teach the proper words and use them from the very beginning. The child who knows that the male sex organ is the penis, that the girl's organ is the vagina, and that water passed from the bladder is urine and not "wee-wee" will not have to unlearn one set of words and learn another when he is older, all the while wondering why his parents did not teach him the true names in the first place." (*Your Child and Sex*, page 30)

Is there a danger that the NEW CREATION program gives children too much too soon?

- The questions that the NEW CREATION series answers in regard to sex and sexuality are the questions young children ask. Since the role of a formal program in catechesis is to support, supplement, and carry forward the education parents are responsible for providing, it is not inappropriate for the program to answer questions the children typically have. Moreover, adults need to be aware that their "too soon" may not be "too soon" for the child. Writing in *Momentum,* Reverend John Forliti notes, "All along the way parents and teachers have to make judgments about what young people are ready for. Too often, the communication between the generations blinds the adults to the youngster's real level of need. Some sex educators believe that a five year gap exists between the time the child has the question and the time the parent thinks he or she has the question. Then, too, many young people recognize that adults in their lives are not able to discuss sex, so they kindly spare them the embarrassment! If mistakes have to be made, I would rather make a mistake in the direction of too much too soon" ("Teaching Sexuality: Confidence is the Key" *Momentum*, May 1982). Monsignor Kelly re-echos what Father Forliti says and points out, "Always instruct your child well ahead of the time you think the information may be needed. Most parents find that it is necessary to repeat a message at least several times before the child fully understands what they are talking about. By the time he encounters the situation you have discussed, he will be prepared to act as you have suggested. In applying this principle, it is well to remember the wise axiom 'Better one year too soon than one second too late.' "

If I am convinced that sex education belongs in the home not in formal instruction programs, what are my rights?

- The NEW CREATION program respects the parents' rights to determine what kind of education in human sexuality their child will receive. The NEW CREATION program concurs with the National Catechetical Directory, "Parents have a right and duty to protest programs which violate their moral and religious convictions. If protests based on well-founded convictions and accurate information are unsuccessful, they have a right to remove their children from the classes, taking care to cause as little embarrassment to the children as possible. Even after their reasonable requirements and specifications have been met, however, some parents remain anxious about education in sexuality. They should not let their feelings express themselves in indiscriminate opposition to all classroom instruction in sexuality, for that would not be consistent with the position of the Second Vatican Council and the Bishops of the United States. (Confer with *To Teach as Jesus Did*, no. 57) Furthermore, to the extent such opposition might impede or disrupt responsible efforts along these lines, it would violate the rights of other, no less conscientious, parents who desire such instruction for their children." (National Catechetical Directory no. 191)

How do I know that the NEW CREATION program is a program that is faithful to Church teaching?

- The program is built upon the guidelines developed by the National Committee for Human Sexuality Education, a committee established in 1981 by the National Conference of Catholic Bishops.
- The program carries an Imprimatur which attests to its faithfulness to Church teaching in the area of faith and morals.
- The program incorporates the goals and guidelines of two educational designs aimed at inculcating Christian values on life-centered issues. These designs were developed under the auspices of the National Catholic Education Association. They are the Respect Life Curriculum Guidelines and Seeking a Just Society.

I want my child to participate in a Christian value-centered approach to catechesis in sexuality. What can I do?

- Participate in planning the program and evaluating it.
- Get to know the teachers in the program.
- Participate in the instruction.
- Communicate with your children who are involved in the program.
- Choose a program which encourages and includes all such forms of parental participation. [NEW CREATION does this.]

(*To Teach as Jesus Did*, no. 59; National Catechetical Directory, no. 191)

# Introduction

Today the question of sexuality education is similar to Mark Twain's comment about the weather. Everybody talks about it but no one seems to know what to do about it. The debate regarding sexuality education usually centers around one or another of these four key issues: *Who* should teach it? *What* should it include? *When* (at what age) should it be presented? *How* should we teach it? Those are the topics we will focus on. We will discuss the relationship between parent and school in providing sexuality education. We will explore and explain the recommended guidelines for a comprehensive program for the seven- to fourteen-year old. We will identify the changing needs of the child for sexuality education as he or she develops during the grade school years. Finally, we will share some ideas on how you as a parent can most effectively go about the task.

This may seem like a tall order, but keep in mind this booklet is only one part of the NEW CREATION program in which your child is participating. Parent sessions will be provided in the overall program to give you an opportunity to review and discuss much of this same information. The students texts at each grade level translate lesson by lesson the *what, how,* and *when* to the child's needs at that level. They also contain home activity suggestions for each lesson that provide practical information on how to present each topic.

This booklet, then, should be approached as one more tool in the program, aimed at giving you a manageable and practical overview of what you need to share with your child and how best to do it. You will want to reread it periodically in the following years to help you adapt your efforts to the changing needs of the child as he or she develops.

# Chapter 1
# Who Is Responsible for Sexuality Education?

In answering the question of who is responsible for providing sexuality education, there is virtually unanimous agreement on one point. Parents or legal guardians have the primary responsibility for this task, just as they have the primary responsibility for all other aspects of the child's nurture and education.

Because it is agreed that parents have this responsibility, it follows that parents have both the moral and civil right to determine what they want their child to know, when it should be presented, and how it should be presented. Parents also have the right to determine who, if anyone, they wish to enlist in helping them fulfill their responsibility.

The laws of the State and the teachings of the Church both agree on these points. They simply reflect the nature of the parent-child relationship as it is understood in our society. As parent or legal guardian you have the final say in the matter of providing sexuality education for your child.

## You Are the Expert

If you are like most other parents, you read this with mixed emotions. You can agree in principle that you are the best person and the most concerned person when it comes to helping your child understand his or her sexuality and embrace it. But you may also feel somewhat awed by the scope of the responsibilities. Maybe you feel somewhat inadequate or ill-prepared to deal with them. There are probably some things you do not feel you fully understand. You may feel somewhat (or very) awkward when it comes to talking about the topic of sexuality, especially as your child grows older.

Because such self-doubts are both natural and understandable, many parents face a temptation quite common in our sophisticated society. Why not turn the task over to "experts"? Sexuality education could be better presented by the doctor or nurse, the teacher, the priest, the people specially trained for such things, one may think.

Regardless of real or imagined inadequacies you may experience, you as parent are the expert when it comes to knowing, understanding, and communicating with your child!

For example, pediatricians have learned to pay close attention to a mother's concern that something is wrong with her baby, even when scientific diagnosis does not immediately reveal any problem. Time and again the mother has preceded modern science's ability to know her child.

Several important studies have shown that throughout childhood and well into the teens, the child continues to look to parents as the primary authority in determining what is right and wrong morally. The influence of parents outranks all other influences including school, peers, and media. So even if parents and guardians are tempted to turn over certain aspects of the child's education and formation to "experts," their own influence remains the dominant one.

Who is in a better position to be aware of the unique needs of your child? Who can better inspire the trust and openness necessary in dealing with delicate and highly personal questions the child will need to ask? Who is in a better position to model the qualities of reverence, appreciation, and self-discipline required in becoming a mature and responsible sexual person? Stated most simply, who loves your child or is more concerned for your child's well-being than you?

## Partners

If sexuality education simply meant imparting biological facts to the child, our whole task would be relatively easy, and it would not make much difference whether the child learned these facts in the home or in the more formal setting of the classroom. Sexuality education is much more than the facts, however. The facts must be rooted in the larger context of a value system and a set of moral convictions. That is what makes sex education in schools such a controversial topic.

In simpler times and in simpler societies this did not present a problem to parents. Society at large tended to support and reinforce the values of individual families. Often, children were surrounded by an extended family of caring adults who shared the values of the parents and helped model and reinforce them among the children. These same values were respected and promoted in the media and in forms of entertainment available to children. It was relatively easy to protect children from being exposed to values contrary to those of the parents.

Today, however, parenting presents a much bigger challenge. Our society is very pluralistic when it comes to moral values. This is most evident in the area of sexuality. You do not have to look very far to find individuals and even organized groups who disagree with you and openly promote sexual values contrary to your own. It is virtually impossible to completely protect your child from being exposed to these contrary values. The media, especially television and movies, permeate our lives and influence our children. It would be a losing battle if you tried to completely protect your child from being exposed to sexual values contrary to your own. Even if you could monitor TV and movies successfully, your child will have friends from families who do not set the same firm standards, and peer influence will sometimes be in direct contradiction to your own values and standards.

One hundred percent protection is not the answer. It is neither possible nor desirable. What is possible and desirable is *minimizing* unsavory influences by reasonable monitoring of free time and *maximizing* the wholesome influence of other adults and peers who share your convictions in the area of sexual morality.

Maximizing wholesome influence is one of the primary reasons parents have for sending a child to a parochial school. Typically, the teachers, whose ongoing influence on your child is undeniable, are adults who share your basic moral convictions. And, to a large extent, your child's classmates will be from families with values similar to your own. The parochial school, unlike its public counterpart, is both allowed and openly committed to promoting the Catholic moral tradition. Its very purpose for existing is to assist, support, and reinforce parents' efforts in imparting their faith and their values to the child.

The parochial school can be aptly described as a kind of "extended family" to your own household, a home away from home which seeks to nurture in your child the same truths and values you promote in the home.

By sponsoring a sexuality education program, such as the NEW CREATION program, the school is not seeking to supplant your parental role. (Nor is it giving you justification for excusing yourself from being personally involved in providing sexuality education.) It is seeking to fulfill a role society at large can no longer be expected to fulfill. It seeks to create an environment which will supplement and reinforce your own home environment. And it seeks to create positive peer influence at the same time.

The Catholic Church, in its official teaching on the matter, is quite clear. It fully recognizes the parent as the primary educator of the child and it also recognizes the parent as having the primary responsibility to provide adequate sexuality education. Neither the school nor any other outside agency has the right to override parents in this matter or to impose an education contrary to the parent's wishes.

Within clearly stated guidelines, however, the parochial school is both allowed and encouraged to provide programs intended to assist the parents in this important task. Programs can and should include classroom instruction by qualified teachers using approved materials. Programs can and should include opportunities for ongoing observation and evaluation by the parents. Programs can and should provide instructional aids and personal instruction directly to parents, as needed, to assist them.

In the area of sexuality education, the parents and the school are best viewed as partners—with the parents being the senior partners.

## The Role of the School

Some parents question whether or not sexuality education, which is a very personal and rather delicate topic, should be taught in the classroom and whether or not children will find it too embarrassing or stressful to talk about in a classroom setting, especially in mixed groups? The point is well made. Some aspects of sexuality education are best discussed in a one-to-one situation with a parent or another trusted adult.

On the other hand, we are social beings and and our sexuality is an integral part of our social nature. Personal sexual values have an impact on our relationships with others. Our sexuality is a concern affecting all of us and all our relationships. We need to be aware of what others think about sexuality and be able to communicate with one another about it. We need to be able to share our convictions and values so we can support one another.

A properly controlled classroom environment can be ideal precisely because it is controlled and directed. It can provide the necessary, respectful atmosphere for children to learn to communicate with one another. It encourages and requires the proper vocabulary. Misunderstandings and misinformation can be readily corrected. Questionable values can be safely challenged.

It is a fact that children will talk about sexuality with one another, often at a much earlier age than most parents realize or want to admit. If we can provide structured classroom opportunities for children to get the proper information and to talk about it together, we eliminate much of their need to do so on the playgrounds, on school buses, or in locker rooms where most of the great myths and errors about human sexuality began and continue to be kept alive.

Much is said about peer influence among children. What is not stressed often enough, however, is that such influence can be a strong positive influence, promoting good values and behavior. It need not be negative. This is important to remember in relation to providing formal programs of sexuality education to children. When children are presented correct information as a group, group influence becomes enlightened. When they are presented with wholesome values and are motivated to pursue them as a group, those values and behaviors become the group norm.

When a teacher presents the proper information to boys and girls together and guides discussion within a respectful, reverent environment, mutual respect and understanding are enhanced. Myths about one another are dispelled, unfounded presumptions about one another's attitudes toward sexuality and sexual behavior are corrected, and natural curiosity is satisfied in a wholesome, informed way. This may sound idealistic, but they remain valid reasons for a sexuality education program that supplements and complements parental instruction with formal classroom instruction. If it were a choice between classroom instruction and parental instruction, there is no question that parental instruction is the choice. But parental instruction supplemented by classroom instruction that is approved by the parents is ideal. It adds a very important and necessary dimension your instruction alone cannot provide—wholesome peer influence and communication.

## Summary

In answering the question of who is responsible for sexuality education, we offer the following conclusions:

1. Parents or legal guardians have the primary right and responsibility to provide education in sexuality for their children.
2. In former times, parents found help in this task from the extended family and to a certain degree from society at large.
3. Today the parochial school is in the best position to assist parents in this important task.
4. Formal classes, approved by parents and properly presented, are an invaluable supplement to parental efforts. Besides the informational aspect, they can promote mutual respect, understanding, and positive support within the child's peer group.

# Chapter 2
# What Are the Goals of Sexuality Education?

If sexuality education was simply a matter of teaching the biology and functions of the human reproductive system, it would be a relatively simple task. But our sexuality embraces more than our capacity to reproduce. Because of the way we human beings are sexual beings, our sexuality is an integral part of who we are as persons. It affects how we think about ourselves, and it has a significant role in all our relationships with others. We cannot really compartmentalize our sexuality or isolate it from the other aspects of our person.

Therefore, what we seek to teach our children about sexuality is not just one-dimensional. It should include moral values, and it will involve the development of our sense of identity and self-worth. Sexuality education should embrace the emotional life, the nature of relationships, and skills for relating. The social roles and vocational choices our sexuality influences should also be considered.

Once we look at sexuality education in this more comprehensive way, we can see that our parental responsibilities can not be limited to having a serious "mother-daughter" or "father-son" talk as the child nears puberty. Our parental responsibility is an ongoing one and will involve both direct and indirect communication, modeling of behavior and attitudes, formal and informal instruction, establishing rules and sanctions, monitoring free time and companions.

Stated that way, it may sound very complicated and a little awesome, but most of what is involved can and will take place in your day-to-day relationship with your child, provided you have some clear ideas of what it is you are trying to achieve. That is the purpose of this chapter: to help you identify the goals for a wholesome and holistic sexuality education for your child.

If the parent's task in sexuality education is multi-dimensional, it should follow that any formal sexuality education provided in a school program will have the same general goals and the same broad scope to it. A class or two on "the facts of life" will not be enough. What is needed will be a comprehensive program that progresses from year to year as the child develops.

That is what the NEW CREATION program seeks to do, in coordination with your own parental efforts.

## The Goals

What, then, are the goals for a comprehensive sexuality education program that both parents and the school could pursue? Fortunately, we have two valuable resources for identifying these goals. The first is a set of guidelines commissioned by the United States Bishops entitled *Education in Human Sexuality*. It was developed in 1981 after consulting with theologians, parents, educators, doctors, and psychologists from throughout the country. The second is the recent document published by the Sacred Congregation for Catholic Education, entitled *Educational Guidance in Human Love: Outline for Sex Education*. (Rome, 1983.)

These are the two major sources used for identifying the goals and developing the content of the NEW CREATION program.

We will present these goals, and the underlying theological principles from which they flow, as they were first presented in *Education in Human Sexuality*. Next, we will examine each one in turn to see the practical implications they have for you as a parent and for a formal sexuality education program. We are suggesting, of course, that you become familiar with them and adopt them as your own goals as you pursue the sexuality education of your child.

## Principles and Goals

Seven theologically-based principles form the foundation for a Christian description of human sexuality:

1. Each person is created unique in the image of God.
2. Despite original sin, all human life in its physical, psychological, and spiritual dimensions is fundamentally good.
3. Each person is created to be loved and to love as Christ, loved by the Father, loves us.

4. Human relationships are expressed in a way that is enfleshed and sexed.
5. Human sexuality carries the responsibility to work toward Christian sexual maturity.
6. Mature Christian sexuality, in whatever state of life, demands a life-enriching commitment to other persons and the community.
7. Conjugal sexuality is an expression of the faithful, life-enriching love of husband and wife and ordained toward the loving procreation of new life.

Corresponding to the seven principles are seven goals:

1. The person will develop a deep appreciation that he or she is a unique reflection of God, and, therefore, possesses inestimable worth.
2. The person will acknowledge and understand the physical, psychological, and spiritual aspects of his or her nature as fundamentally good.
3. The person will be open to receive love and will love others in accord with his or her level of maturation.
4. The person will be open to the growth which takes place within interpersonal life and will participate in relationships as a sexual person in accord with his or her own state of life.
5. The person will appreciate the responsibility demanded in the transition from immature self-centeredness to mature Christian altruism and generosity.
6. The person will appreciate the role played by sexuality in establishing relationships of commitment and fidelity.
7. The person will appreciate the fundamental purposes of Christian marriage by affirming the mutually related unitive and procreative ends of this sacramental relationship.

A summary of the seven principles may be useful in providing an overall sense of their dynamism and comprehensiveness. It may be stated that the goal of Christian catechesis in sexuality is to communicate effectively that the person is unique, good, loved and loving, sexual, responsible, committed, and, if married, exclusively faithful and procreative. The following chart may help to capsulize the principles and goals:

## General Principle

1. Each person is created unique in the image of God.

   **Goal:** The person will develop a deep appreciation that he or she is a unique reflection of God, and, therefore, possesses inestimable worth.

   **Summary:** unique

2. Even though original sin has weakened our human nature, making us imperfect and susceptible to temptation and personal sin, all human life in its physical, psychological, and spiritual dimensions is fundamentally good.

   **Goal:** The person will acknowledge and understand the physical, psychological, and spiritual aspects of his or her nature and appreciate them as fundamentally good, though imperfect.

   **Summary:** good, though imperfect

3. Each person is created to be loved and to love as Christ, loved by the Father, loves us.

   **Goal:** The person will be open to receive love and will love others in accord with his or her level of maturation.

   **Summary:** loved and loving

4. Human relationships are expressed in a way that is enfleshed and sexed.

   **Goal:** The person will be open to the growth which takes place within interpersonal life, and will participate in relationships as a sexual person in accord with his or her own state of life.

   **Summary:** sexual

5. Human sexuality carries the responsiblity to work toward Christian sexual maturity.

   **Goal:** The person will appreciate the responsibility demanded in the transition from immature self-centeredness to mature Christian altruism and generosity.

   **Summary:** responsible

6. Mature Christian sexuality, in whatever state of life, demands a life-enriching commitment to other persons and the community.

   **Goal:** The person will appreciate the role played by sexuality in establishing relationships of commitment and fidelity.

   **Summary:** committed

7. Conjugal sexuality is an expression of the faithful, life-enriching love of husband and wife and is ordained toward the loving procreation of new life.

   **Goal:** The person will appreciate the fundamental purpose of Christian marriage by affirming the mutually related unitive and procreative ends of this sacramental relationship.

   **Summary:** faithful and procreative[1]

# Exploring the Goals

Before examining each of these goals in more detail, please keep in mind they describe the "what" of sexuality education in terms of the scope of sexuality education in the general sense, regardless of the age of the child. The "What" in terms of identifying *specific* content to be presented at a given age level (e.g., the menstrual cycle, the stages of pregnancy, the morality of nonmarital sexual intercourse) is considered in the next chapter which deals with the question, "When is the child ready for what?"

---

1. *Education in Human Sexuality for Christians* (Washington, D.C.: United States Catholic Conference, 1981), pp. 6–8.

## Goal One

The child will develop a deep appreciation that he or she is a unique reflection of God, and therefore possesses inestimable worth.

**Parenting Focus:** Seek to continue to nurture in your child a sense of his or her specialness and self-worth. You do this in an ongoing way each time you express love, affirmation, and concern for your child in ways he or she can recognize.

**Rationale:** At the heart of Jesus' message is the good news that each person is special and specially loved by the Father. Being convinced of this will be the source of the individual's self-esteem. It also becomes the motive for avoiding any behavior that would be a betrayal of one's dignity. By extension, this same conviction becomes the basis for the respect we show for the dignity of others.

In relation to sexuality education, the importance of this goal is rather obvious. Our sexuality is an integral part of what makes us unique and special in the eyes of God. It is one of the sources for the dignity and worth we possess. If a child can be helped to discover and become convinced of this, it is hardly likely that he or she will treat sexuality lightly or view it as something burdensome or shameful. In the same way, the child will have the foundations for treating others with respect, rather than as "sex objects" to be used or manipulated for personal gain.

Nurturing this kind of self-esteem and awareness of personal dignity is one of the most basic goals of parenting. It is not something special to sexuality education. A sense of self-worth is the foundation for all aspects of human development. Wholesome, psychological, moral, social, and even physical development have their roots in this sense of self-esteem.

As a parent, you promote this sense of self-esteem and personal dignity in an ongoing way at each stage of your child's growth from infancy onward. You do not have to give it a particularly sexual focus to be effective. However, as we will see, there are stages in the child's development when you will want to more directly reinforce the conviction that sexuality is an integral part of what makes him or her lovable and precious in the eyes of God.

Consider this goal foundational and pervasive for you as a parent. Whatever you do to nurture this sense of personal worth and dignity will have a significant role to play in the overall sexual education of your child.

It is also difficult, if not impossible, to "teach" this in a classroom. The child's sense of personal worth will be "caught" more than "taught." A classroom program can reinforce and explain the concept, but the conviction of personal worth must be nurtured within the family on a day-to-day basis. In doing that, you are always involved in sexuality education of your child in one of the best possible ways.

## Goal Two

The child will acknowledge and understand the physical, psychological, and spiritual aspects of his or her nature and appreciate them as fundamentally good though imperfect.

**Parenting Focus** Seek to share information about sexuality with your child in as balanced a manner as possible. While continually stressing the fundamental goodness of sexuality as created by God, you will want to maintain a compassionate realism regarding our human frailties and limitations.

**Rationale:** In teaching specifics about sexuality, the overall tone and attitude should always be positive and reverent. You cannot overemphasize or repeat too often that human sexuality is a gift from God. Continually seek to help the child embrace it gratefully as the wonderful gift God intends it to be.

At the same time, we cannot escape the fact that God's creation has become contaminated by sin. Though we are redeemed in Jesus and participate in building the New Creation as sexed and sexual persons, the potential for misusing our gift remains. This note of realism needs to be included in sexuality education efforts, in keeping with the child's developing capacity to understand it.

Help the developing child realize that human sexuality is good and, yet, can sometimes be troublesome and a source of temptation. Therefore, the key to understanding this goal of sexuality education is balance. A balanced approach eliminates naiveté and ignorance on one hand and fear and negativism on the other.

## Goal Three

The child will be open to receive love and will love others in accord with his or her level of maturation.

**Parenting Focus** Seek to help the child become comfortable in both expressing and receiving love in keeping with his or her stage of development. Your own frequent and concrete expressions of affection within the family and in particular those you direct toward your child will nurture this quality.

**Rationale** Being open to receive love and being able to love unselfishly is a sign of wholesome sexual maturity. Hence, it is one of the central goals of sexuality education. We are not speaking of love, of course, just in the narrow sense of its genital expression. We are speaking of it in the deeper, spiritual sense as selflessness and authentic concern for others. Genital love is only one form it takes.

This goal, therefore, involves two things. The first and most important is providing the child with the ongoing experience of being loved within the family and providing the child with opportunities to express love in turn. That you seek to do this is taken for granted. How you actually do this, as we will see later, can play a very important role in your child's overall development as a mature sexual person.

The second part of this goal is intellectual as well as experiential. We must help the child both understand and be able to recognize the difference between authentic expressions of love and those selfish, self-seeking relationships that sometimes are popularly described as love. This becomes a more and more important aspect of the goal as the child enters and moves through puberty toward adulthood. But throughout the child's development the frequent manifestations of your own love for him or her is one of the most direct ways to foster this dimension of sexuality education.

## Goal Four

The child will be open to growth which takes place within interpersonal life, and will participate in relationships as a sexual person in accord with his or her own life state.

**Parenting Focus** Share with your child the necessary factual information about human sexuality, the biology of the human reproductive system, and the nature of reproduction.

Seek to do this within the context of your own moral values and your own deep appreciation and reverence for the gift of sexuality.

**Rationale** Sharing "the facts of life" with the child is obviously an integral part of sexuality education. Your child will need to know, in more and more detail as he or she develops, what it means to be male and female. Your child will need to understand and appreciate the nature and function of his or her own body and its reproductive system. In the same way, the child will need to understand and appreciate the reproductive system of the other sex.

As the goal states, we are oriented toward an interpersonal life and toward entering into relationships as sexual persons. Therefore, we can never treat the "facts of life" abstractly or as totally divorced from moral values. We cannot totally isolate the facts about sexuality from personal relationships since all personal relationships have a sexual dimension.

It is a relatively easy task to teach your child biological terms and to describe the various functions of the parts of the reproductive system. It is relatively easy to determine when your child should be presented with certain facts, in keeping with the ongoing maturing process. The real challenge this goal presents to you as a parent and to professional educators also is to ensure that your child can make the connection between abstract facts about sex and real persons who possess sexual natures. That is, we must help the child see these facts at work within the self and within the everyday relationships he or she experiences.

In addition, as the next goal suggests, these same facts, as important as they are in themselves to an understanding of sexuality, must be seen in connection with the moral responsibilities they entail.

As a parent, then, one of your goals in sexuality education will be to ensure that your child receives the factual information he or she needs. But this factual information must be personalized for your child, and it needs to be presented against the backdrop of the interpersonal relationships which make up our lives as humans.

# Goal Five

The child will appreciate the responsibility demanded in the transition from immature self-centeredness to mature Christian altruism and generosity.

**Parenting Focus:** Simply stated, seek to communicate to your child your own sense of right and wrong in the area of sexual morality and sexual behavior.

**Rationale:** Some parents might be tempted to think that if they could just teach their child what is right and wrong morally in the area of sexual behavior—and get the child to follow it—that's all the sex education that is needed.

Unfortunately, it is not quite that simple. Moral development, in general, is a delicate and rather complex process. There is still much we do not understand about how it takes place. Teaching sexual morality, in particular, can in some ways be even more difficult. This is partly true because of the moral pluralism in society today. There are many different approaches to sexual morality being proclaimed, some of which are in direct contradiction to our Judeo-Christian tradition. You will have competition in trying to teach your own values to your child.

Your child may never have to face tough personal choices involving acts like murder or robbery. Those are not everyday situations, so he or she may find it easy to accept the moral principles governing those acts. But as your child develops he or she may have to face moral decisions related to sexual behavior frequently, even on a day-to-day basis. This means your child will have many opportunities to apply—and therefore challenge and test—the moral principles you promote in the area of sexuality.

That is why, as a parent, it will never be enough to simply say something is wrong "because it is a sin" or "because I say you cannot." Naming certain acts sins is valid and necessary. It is also necessary and valid to set down rules you expect to be followed. But it is equally important that you seek to develop the overall understanding, appreciation, and personal attitudes toward sexuality that are implied in all seven goals of sexuality education. You will find it impossible to achieve this goal if you are not at the same time pursuing the other six goals because they are all interrelated. If you are successfully fostering the other goals, it will be easier and you will be more successful in achieving the goal of fostering moral responsibility.

At the core of a Christian understanding of sexuality is a profound appreciation and respect for its goodness as a gift from God. It is this appreciation and respect that will ultimately motivate responsible behavior.

Misuse of our sexual powers is always a serious matter in principle and will often have serious consequences. In keeping with your child's ability to understand, you will want to help him or her realize this. At the same time, be careful not to stress fear or guilt as the primary motive for responsible sexual behavior. The underlying motive to foster in promoting responsible behavior should be that of respect and appreciation for our sexuality in all its dimensions. That involves pursuing all the goals of the NEW CREATION program, not just goal five.

## Goal Six

The child will appreciate the role played by sexuality in establishing relationships of commitment and fidelity.

**Parenting Focus:** Seek to nurture in your child the awareness that our sexuality is intended to be creative and life-giving in all relationships and walks of life, not just within the married state. This requires that they learn to exercise fidelity and commitment in the relationships they experience as they grow.

**Rationale:** The developing child needs your help in understanding the creative potential his or her sexuality can bring to all relationships, not just the husband-wife relationship. At the same time, the child will need to understand that no relationship can be fruitful or creative if the qualities of commitment and fidelity are missing.

All relationships need the stability of commitment and fidelity to enjoy the creative and life-giving effect our sexuality is designed to achieve. This is true of friendships. It is true in celibate ministry, such as priesthood. And it is true within the fellowship of faith community, such as a parish. So it is not just the married relationship that can be made creative and fruitful because of our sexuality. Nor is it just the married relationship that will require commitment and fidelity.

It is obvious that the full meaning of this dimension of our sexuality will remain beyond the grasp of the child for some time. You cannot hope to teach it as a formal concept until the early teens. But throughout childhood, you can foster the qualities of loyalty and commitment—to family, to Church, to friends, to groups and organizations the child joins. And you can help your child see that it is these qualities that create successful, fruitful relationships. At first, this may not seem to have much direct bearing on sexuality education but its importance as a goal in sexuality education becomes evident when you expand your understanding of the life-giving purpose of sexuality beyond its physical, genital sense. Our sexuality's life-giving potential includes life in all its forms: spiritual, emotional, intellectual, and communal. When seen in that light, you can realize that nurturing the qualities of fidelity and commitment in your child is an integral part of his or her sexuality education.

## Goal Seven

The child will appreciate the fundamental purposes of Christian marriage by affirming the mutually important unitive and procreative ends of this sacramental relationship.

**Parenting Focus:** By word and example, seek to lay the foundations for understanding and appreciating the nature of sacramental marriage. Help your child develop those skills in relating and those attitudes upon which successful marriages are built. At the same time, be honest in sharing the difficulties and challenges the vocation of marriage and parenting present to every couple.

**Rationale:** At the grade school level, it is premature to equate marriage preparation with this goal. At best, the goal implies remote preparation only. But it is possible throughout childhood to develop a sense of the beauty and purpose of marriage, as well as a sense of realism toward what the marriage commitment can entail.

A basic goal of the holistic program of sexuality education for your child will include nurturing an understanding and appreciation for the married state, in keeping with the plan of God and the teaching of the Church.

As the child's capacity to understand develops, this goal includes a more formal education in the Church's teachings regarding marriage and the rationale of the laws that govern the sacrament. This task can be handled effectively in a classroom setting, but you are expected to support these efforts by showing your own loyalty to the Church and your own commitment to the ideals contained in the Gospel.

Today, you will find both misunderstanding and controversy surrounding some of the Church's teachings on marriage and related issues (e.g., divorce, annulment). Therefore, it is important that you first clarify your understanding of what the Church is actually teaching. Also, it will be important for you to deal with any personal differences you may have regarding the Church's teaching and your own moral convictions. Until you have resolved important issues in your own mind, you cannot hope to be successful in helping your child.

## Summary

You should find it somewhat encouraging as a parent to realize that most of the goals of sexuality education are closely connected with your overall efforts to parent. They do not demand that you do new things as much as they require that you continue what you already are doing as a parent. You are only being asked to do these things with a new degree of sensitivity and awareness. Knowledge of these goals should help you recognize the many regular, even daily opportunities you have to enhance the child's understanding and appreciation of his or her sexuality and its pervasive role in our lives.

The seven goals are summarized by these seven phrases:

1. Unique
2. Good, though imperfect
3. Loved and loving
4. Sexual
5. Responsible
6. Committed
7. Faithful and procreative

That list expresses the "what" of sexuality education. It describes "what" kind of understanding and "what" kind of attitudes you should seek to develop in your child in an ongoing way. The more familiar you can become with them and the rationale behind them, the more readily you will recognize the opportunities you have in the normal course of family life to promote them in your child.

At the same time, they represent the heart of the NEW CREATION program being taught in your child's school.

These seven goals are pursued each year of the program, in keeping with the child's readiness and need at each grade level. It will be helpful to relate these goals to each of the lessons in the student text. In this way, you can better understand "what" is being taught at any given time and why. The student text for each grade is designed as follows:

- Lessons one and two—Goal one: Unique
- Lessons three and four—Goal two: Good, though Imperfect
- Lessons five and six—Goal three: Loved and Loving
- Lessons seven and eight—Goal four: Sexual
- Lessons nine and ten—Goal five: Responsible
- Lessons eleven and twelve—Goal six: Committed
- Lessons thirteen and fourteen—Goal seven: Faithful and Procreative

Obviously, your own parenting efforts cannot be arranged in such precise order. Opportunities for promoting any particular goal may occur at any time, but it is good to know that each year the NEW CREATION program will give you many opportunities to address each goal in a more formal and precise way as a specific goal is being treated in the lesson for that week. By coordinating your efforts with those of the formal classes, you will be able to give special attention to each goal each year.

# Chapter 3
# When to Teach What

For most parents, the question of "when" to teach "what" is a primary concern. It is also a very practical concern. How old should the child be before we explain "where babies come from?" When is the best age to begin explaining about things like venereal disease? How much information (if any) about birth control should the child have by the time he or she reaches high school? When is the right age to begin to explain about menstruation?

There are two things you have to consider in seeking to translate the general goals or the "what" as they are described in chapter two into the specific topics, facts, and information that should be presented at specific ages in the child's growth.

## 1. The Readiness of the Child

By readiness, we mean the age at which the child's intellectual capacity develops to the point where he or she is able to understand and deal with certain kinds of information in a formal or systematic way. For example, it is often possible to give a six- or seven-year-old a simple explanation of "where babies come from" without going into great detail. It is all the child is ready to understand and, usually, all the child needs to know. But the ten- or eleven-year-old will be ready for and able to handle the explanation that is much more scientifically precise. In the same way, the six- or seven-year-old is not ready for or able to understand the moral implications of certain kinds of sexual behavior, such as the harmfulness of pornography. The typical twelve-year-old will be ready.

Readiness also involves the child's psychological readiness. Even though a child may be ready in the intellectual sense of being able to understand certain things, that does not mean the child is always psychologically ready to deal with them. How can you as a parent know when your child is ready for what? Fortunately, there is general agreement regarding the stages of development the children go through during the grade school years, which make it possible to predict, rather accurately, the child's general intellectual and psychological readiness to deal with certain kinds of information at any given age. Much of this chapter is devoted to thumbnail sketches describing these stages and their implications for sexuality education.

The student texts at each grade level of the NEW CREATION program have been developed in keeping with this knowledge. New or more detailed information is introduced at those grade levels when it is generally agreed the children are ready to deal with it effectively. It will be helpful to you to become familiar with the material that is presented at each grade level as your child enters that grade. It will give you a good sense both of what the child should be ready for and the degree of detail he or she is ready to handle.

## 2. The Needs of the Child

There are two kinds of needs the child will experience in relation to sexuality education. The first need is dictated by the child's normal development. For example, as girls near puberty and the beginning of menstruation, they will need to be prepared for this. In a similar way, boys nearing puberty will need to know about nocturnal emissions (wet dreams). It is fairly easy to anticipate needs of this kind since the child's development is fairly predictable. The material in the NEW CREATION program seeks to anticipate such needs by introducing appropriate information in keeping with the child's stage of development at a given grade level.

The NEW CREATION program will not introduce such material *too soon*. So the text at any grade level will be your cue to deal with that material in the home situation also. However, it may happen that your child is developing "ahead of schedule" physically. Being alert to this, you may want to deal with some topics, like menstruation, before the program introduces them or in more detail than when they are covered at a given grade level. While the development of children at certain stages is predictable in a general sense, each child remains unique. You, as parent, are in the best position to judge if your child needs information that has not yet been introduced in the program.

A second kind of need the child will experience can be described as "ad hoc." A good example of this is the toddler who needs to know why Mommie (who is pregnant) is getting so fat. In other words, particular circumstances and situations will trigger a need to know some specific information from time to time. The need is usually expressed in the form of a question. Even if a question is not asked, you, as parent, can sometimes recognize the need to deal with some topic because of an experience the child has had.

A typical event that can trigger an "ad hoc" need to know may be the child observing dogs or other animals copulating. Or the child may overhear a word used on the playground and want to know what it means. Stories seen on TV and events covered in newscasts can raise questions in the child's mind. In today's society occasions for triggering questions abound. It is an unfortunate fact, but children should be taught at an early age to recognize sexual abuse in order to protect themselves. This is a topic you as parents will want to initiate, since it is a need the child will not feel. Also, you will want to deal with divorce if it occurs within the family or among friends, even if the child is unable to or hesitant about raising these questions.

In the next chapter, we will discuss some proven ways to deal with the questions the children raise and how to initiate discussion on topics they need to know about. For now, it is enough to be aware that you cannot fully program your child's sexuality education. You will have to be ready to respond on an "ad hoc" basis from time to time as questions arise. You will have to be alert to initiate discussion on topics if an occasion warrants it, even if the child is unable to express his or her need.

## Stages of Development: Sketches of the Grade School Child

What follows are thumbnail sketches of the chief characteristics and needs of children as they progress through the three distinct stages of development embraced by the NEW CREATION program (grades 1–8). If you are at all familiar with current theories of child development, much of what is presented will be familiar to you. In addition, your own experience, gained from observing your child's development, will be borne out.

As you read these sketches, keep in mind that they are only intended as a *general* picture of children in each age group. Your child remains unique and his or her development will always have some unique aspects to it. This fact reinforces once again the principle that you will want to remain actively involved in the sexuality education of your child at each stage. No one is in a better position to recognize and appreciate the unique qualities and needs of your child than you are.

After the description of each age group, we will list some specific objectives and topics related to sexuality education that are appropriate for parents to pursue for that age group. They are derived from *Education in Human Sexuality*, the United States Bishops' guidelines on sexuality education. The descriptions can give you a good overview of the kinds of information and attitudes you will want to focus on in working with your child at that stage of development.

# Primary Level (*Ages 6–8, Grades 1–3*)

## Intellectual Development

Children at this stage are able to reason at the concrete level. It is only at the end of this stage that they become able to deal with abstract relationships (general principles). Reading, writing, and basic math skills fascinate them and give them a sense of control to the degree they begin to master them. Of equal interest, however, is the physical world, especially anything related to living things, growth and how things function. They have uninhibited curiosity about the processes of human development and physical growth, especially their own. They can also begin to recognize and distinguish between the various emotions they experience and can begin to see the need to exercise some control over them.

## Social Development

The child will still tend to be primarily self-centered, but can share on a reciprocal basis. Concern for others develops gradually. The child needs reminders and opportunities to exercise such concern. It does not usually come naturally at this stage. As they become more self-conscious, children at this stage will need more direct reinforcement of self-esteem, especially from you and from other significant adults. Praise, approval, and other positive forms of encouragement for their efforts are vital to them. The need for peer approval begins to intensify toward the end of this stage, but the approval, love, and support of parents and significant adults remains the dominant influence in the development of self-esteem. Family relationships remain the major influence in the development of social skills and in the understanding of social roles. Play is also an important means for the child to experiment and to try various roles and kinds of social behavior. Play will gradually give way to "real world" relationships with peers toward the end of this stage.

## Moral Development

Development at this stage still focuses on self-interest. The simple principle of reward and punishment remains the basic motive for proper behavior. The child is still too young to grasp moral principles, as such, or the rationale behind them. Your guidance comes basically by providing clear rules and specific, consistent sanctions or punishment when he or she breaks them. Later in this stage, the child becomes more aware of the significance of behavior in terms of the rights of others and in terms of the effects of certain kinds of behavior on persons. This kind of moral awareness will continue to unfold gradually throughout childhood and into adolescence.

## Sexual Development

There is a natural but almost detached interest in information involving anatomy and related topics. Interest and curiosity about sexual matters is on the same plane as interest and curiosity about any other aspects of the body or about the world around them. Interest will be expressed in a naive, uninhibited, and straightforward manner in most cases. Curiosity is shown in terms of specific things the child hears or notices, rather than in terms of a need for systematic and detailed information that has significant personal value or application. Boys and girls can play together quite freely without being self-conscious. Differences between boys and girls are taken for granted. For the most part, attention to differences focuses on superimposed or sociological differences such as difference in dress, interest, or in play. At this level, there is a natural tendency for some boys and girls to prefer to separate socially and to occasionally express a distinct dislike for the other sex such as "I hate boys."

## Specific Objectives for This Age Level (*Ages 6-8*)

The child will:

1. be helped to see the value of friendship and loyalty;
2. experience support in the face of personal failures;
3. be supported and encouraged to dialogue openly and freely about experiences outside the home;
4. be given an opportunity to solve some problems alone;
5. understand the responsibilities to contribute positively to his or her own family life;
6. experience a reinforcement of authentic religious ideas and values within the home;
7. appreciate forgiveness in the home as an expression of Christian forgiveness;
8. develop a capacity for tolerating and appreciating differences in others;
9. explore family history and the family's unique identity;
10. begin to differentiate positive from negative societal sexual influences;
11. be given an appreciation of positive heroic figures;
12. be given an opportunity for ongoing interaction with a father figure;
13. be given an experience of direct warmth and closeness from the same sex parent;
14. gain a basic understanding of menstruation and sexual intercourse if called for at this age level;
15. be given adequate information, with proper terminology, regarding questions of a sexual nature which arise from natural curiosity;
16. appreciate the parental need for privacy.[1]

## Specific Topics to Be Introduced at This Age Level (*Ages 6–8*)

The child will:

1. learn about his or her body and how to care for it.
2. be taught the proper terminology for naming the parts of the male and female reproductive systems and be given a basic understanding of their functions.
3. understand the cooperative role of parents in the conception and nurturing of new human life.

## Intermediate Level (*Ages 9–11, Grades 4–6*)

## Intellectual Development

The significant growth at this level is in the capacity for deductive reasoning. Children can begin to take a general rule or principle and apply it to specific situations. This capacity unfolds gradually, however, and will not be fully developed until the next stage. For the most part, this stage is still an information-gathering stage. Interest in the material universe and in science increases. The child gets a sense of control over the world by being able to organize it into categories and to predict outcomes by applying the laws he or she discovers and is taught.

Hobbies often involve collecting things—stamps, coins, matchbook covers, stickers, etc. The child can spend hours reviewing and reorganizing his or her treasures. This interest is symbolic of what is taking place internally. The child is collecting, storing, and organizing a wide amount of data about his or her world. But the child does not yet have the capacity or interest for making subtle distinctions or for forming a clear hierarchy of values. This capacity and interest emerges later.

---

1. *Education in Human Sexuality* (Washington, DC: United States Catholic Conference, 1981), pp. 27–28.

## Social Development

Peers and friends begin to absorb more of the child's interest and time. Peer influence increases, but family relationships and influence continue to dominate. In learning and assuming social roles and proper modes of behavior, modeling by you and other significant adults continues to play the key part, but older siblings, older children in the school environment, and media personalities have a definite influence also. Boy-girl relationships gradually become more self-conscious, and boys and girls tend to naturally segregate at the social level. However, in more structured situations such as on teams, in classes, and the like, they can work and play together quite naturally. Though still basically self-centered, children can begin to appreciate the need and value of fair play, cooperation, and loyalty in relationships. They tend to be more prone to cry "foul" than to admit a "foul" in their relationships, but they are beginning to recognize the need for rules.

## Moral Development

The child's development is somewhat parallel to the intellectual and social development taking place. Motivation shifts from fear of punishment to that of winning the approval of others for proper behavior. Approval from parents and other significant adults is more important than approval from peers. Positive reinforcement and praise for proper behavior are to be a central feature of moral formation at the beginning of this stage. Gradually, however, as the child's capacity for appreciating the logic of rules increases, "keeping the rules" for their own sake takes on more importance as a motivating factor. It is important for you during this stage to explain the logic behind rules as much as possible. In doing so, however, we must keep in mind the fact that the child is still quite limited and cannot grasp abstract principles. Fair play will make sense. Concepts like mercy remain beyond the grasp of children even if they can learn the definitions for the terms.

## Sexual Development

The child's interest and need for more systematic information keeps pace with the same desire to gather data and to organize it that marks the overall intellectual growth of the child. The interest has a more personal application than in the earlier stage, but the child is still somewhat detached. At the start the child is interested primarily in studying *the* body, and only to a lesser degree in studying his or her body. Information and specific facts gathered earlier now need to be organized in a more systematic way by the child. Gradually in some, more rapidly in others, information about sexuality takes on much more personal significance and a more self-conscious quality. This will obviously be the case for the children who begin to enter puberty during the middle or end of this stage. For this reason, sexuality education in the school must be presented in an increasingly formal and direct manner. In the home, you need to be sensitive to this shift from detached interest to the wonderful but sometimes frightening personal implications of what the child is discovering about his or her *own* body, rather than *the* body. You not only have a direct and very important role in imparting information during this stage, you also have the critical task of reassuring and affirming the goodness of the developing sexuality as puberty approaches.

## Specific Objectives for This Age Level (*Ages 9–11*)

The preadolescent will:

1. appreciate the different rates of sexual maturation and be assured of the normalcy of his or her own rate of change;
2. feel encouragement in developing a spirit of toleration for self and for the differences perceived in others;
3. learn the proper terminology related to psycho-sexual functioning and discuss sexual intercourse with parents or someone entrusted by their parents;
4. discuss in group settings or with parents basic Christian principles related to sexuality;
5. be provided with opportunities for relating to the opposite sex in a nonthreatening way;
6. exercise the critical ability to evaluate the marketplace-understanding of sexuality;

7. experience support even when there has been personal failure;
8. experience the value of personal privacy;
9. develop certain patterns of familial responsibility by freely contributing to the tasks and functions of the family;
10. understand and discuss some of the virtues essential to friendship such as loyalty, responsibility;
11. appreciate that God's love accepts us as we are and as we change;
12. reflect on the presence of Christ in their daily lives.[2]

## Specific Topics to Be Introduced at This Age Level (*Ages 9–11*)

The topics identified here are not intended to be exhaustive of the full scope of sexuality education at this age level. Those listed focus only on the kind of factual information related to sexuality which are to be presented and explained. The child will:

1. understand his/her own developing body: male and female reproductive systems, puberty, physical sex characteristics, chemical changes, menstruation, physical attraction and responses, the nature of sexual intercourse, etc.
2. understand the emotional changes accompanying puberty. E.g., sensitivity, enthusiasm, mood swings, anger, boredom, etc.
3. understand why sexual intercourse and reproduction should be limited to the married state.
4. be given criteria for evaluating the sexual values presented in contemporary media: music, TV, movies, etc.
5. become aware of the harmfulness of sexual stereotypes and sexual discrimination.

---

2. *Education in Human Sexuality*, p. 30.

# Junior High (*Ages 12-14, Grades 7-8*)

## Intellectual Development

The child's capacity for logic and deductive thinking reaches almost the adult level during this stage. However, the child is still not able to fully operate at the level of the abstract or spiritual. Given the capacity for logic and deductive reason, the child is not satisfied with answers like "because mother or father says" and will want answers that he or she can understand.

The child finds it necessary to challenge and re-examine many truths, rules, and laws that before had been accepted on your word only. The child is becoming rapidly more self-conscious at the same time and shows a great deal of interest in learning about the self, both emotional and physical. Physical sciences also interest this age group, as does history, if it focuses on "real people" and not just on impersonal facts and events.

## Social Development

The child begins to feel a stronger need to move beyond the family and to form relationships with peers. Peer influence becomes a significant factor both in forming ideas and in behavior and can be in direct competition to parental ideas and values. The child will begin to prefer the companionship of peers to that of family and will often express embarrassment if you show affection or concern toward them in front of their peers. Basically, the child is seeking to break out of his or her "child image" and makes the first tentative steps toward authentic independence. Having no strong sense of an interiorized self-identity, the child depends to a large extent on using the peer group for this identity. Clothing, hairstyle, and other externals become very important. The standards are set mostly by the peer group and by what they judge to be socially "in."

Both boys and girls usually feel awkward and self-conscious in one-to-one relationships with someone of the opposite sex, but they can enjoy mixed company if it is of a group nature. There is a strong natural tendency toward same sex grouping at this age since it gives the individual a sense of support and helps the child form his or her own sexual identity as a male or female. Typically, girls develop more rapidly than boys in all areas during this stage. Therefore, they may tend to appear or be more socially mature than boys the same age.

## Moral Development

The child is now able to more fully understand the rationale of various moral principles and to see that responsibility for actions extends beyond immediate effects to the more indirect or long-range effects of their choices. However, they still tend to focus only on immediate results as the basis for judging the goodness or badness of an act. You will need to constantly remind them to think about consequences beyond the immediate.

They approach morality more on a legal and logical level than in terms of ideals and first principles. They expect all laws and rules to be both fair and reasonable and will challenge any that do not seem to fit that criteria. For example, they might be able to explain a Gospel virtue like "turning the other cheek" but are not yet capable of interiorizing it since it does not seem quite fair or reasonable. For this reason, the child is prone to challenge various moral principles and rules you uphold. As much as possible it is important for you to take the time to demonstrate in practical terms the fairness and logic of the moral principles being presented and promoted. It is not enough in most instances to simply say "because I told you so" or "the Church says." This tendency to challenge and to demand reasons for everything, though quite aggravating at times, is actually a wholesome and necessary step toward understanding and interiorizing values that have been only external to them in earlier childhood. At the same time, it will be necessary for you to be firm in demanding conformity to certain rules and principles even if you cannot adequately explain them at the level of logic. Some truths go beyond either the boundaries of logic or our own ability to argue. At this stage, nonagreement can never be allowed as an excuse for disobedience, no matter how much the child may protest at the time. Clear, consistent, and firm parental authority remains an important element in the moral formation at this stage. As much as possible, apply it calmly and with patience.

# Sexual Development

This is a very important stage in the child's development, because he or she has begun, or probably will begin, to experience the physical and emotional changes of puberty during this time. We cannot stress too often, however, that each child will develop at his or her own pace according to a personal body clock. Some children, girls more often than boys, will have begun puberty in the middle grades. Some children, boys more often than girls, may not actually begin puberty until age fourteen or even later. There is no need to worry or cause the child to worry if he or she is ahead of or behind the other children in the class or peer group.

Volumes have been written describing puberty and its physical and emotional development. In the NEW CREATION program, the groundwork for understanding puberty is laid in the intermediate grades and developed quite fully in sixth, seventh, and eighth grades. Being familiar with the content of the program at each grade level will be a great help to you in expanding and reinforcing what is being presented to the child. The biological changes that take place are rather easy to present and to understand. When the child is helped to understand the changes, he or she may still be confused or unsettled by the actual experience, but the changes will seem more wholesome and natural. At the emotional level, however, the child will usually experience some degree of personal turmoil no matter how much information he or she has. Swift changes in emotions, for no apparent reason, are common. Emotions related to self-image are usually quite strong.

Physical awkwardness and body awareness intensify and often exaggerate self-consciousness. Self-esteem can suffer. Both boys and girls need a great deal of tangible affirmation and reassurance from you. Studying about body changes is one thing. Experiencing them is quite another. The child needs to be told over and over in tangible ways that he or she is "okay." Interest in the other sex takes on a new dimension at this stage. It is a kind of "love-hate" relationship. Curiosity and feelings of attraction are quite common, but there can also be a kind of natural aversion to members of the other sex. Lacking a firm self-identity as a male or female, the child can feel threatened or awkward around the other sex. Doubts about one's sexual identity are not uncommon but usually superficial.

Appropriate role-modeling by you and other significant adults plays an important part in helping the child form his or her own identity and assume appropriate roles. Role-modeling has been important throughout childhood, but assumes a purposefulness at this stage. Conscious father-son and mother-daughter relationships begin to play a more important part during this formative stage and will continue to be important through adolescence. If you are a solo parent, it is a good idea to involve other significant adults who can supply the missing role-model and companionship for the child. At this stage, girls often tend to mature at a more advanced pace than boys. While it is up to you to set your own rules in regard to dating, a good principle to follow is this: do not be in any hurry and do not put pressure on the child. An interest in the other sex develops according to the individual child's timetable. It is quite normal for some children to have no interest in dating relationships until the late teens. This should be no cause for alarm. Pressuring the child into "becoming interested" can retard rather than promote a wholesome sexual identity and wholesome relationships. On the other hand, it may be necessary to apply parental restraints on the child who shows a too precocious interest in the other sex. The interest may be authentic and quite normal, but the child still lacks the necessary maturity of judgment and self-discipline for an unsupervised and unregulated relationship.

## Specific Objectives for This Age Level (*Ages 12–14*)

The adolescent will:

1. be given more responsibilities both within and outside the home;
2. exercise a greater range of decision-making with regards to self, other persons, and possessions;
3. interact with nonparental adults and join in some adult celebrations;
4. appreciate the dignity of all persons regardless of age, social position, race, or religion;

5. experience a climate in the home where family and social values can be discussed with candor and mutual respect;
6. be given initial guidance in the experience of dating;
7. discuss and understand the meaning and responsibility of sexual intercourse;
8. be aware of some of the dangers of sexual experimentation;
9. appreciate the dignity of procreation and the responsibilities accompanying the creating of new life;
10. feel support and kindness for any awkwardness experienced in girl/boy relating;
11. appreciate the value of modesty and privacy;
12. sense the continuing value of religion and religious practices in the home;
13. experience a climate of tolerance and support for developing individuality at home;
14. express discernment concerning the marketplace view of sexuality.[3]

## Specific Topics to be Introduced at This Age Level (*Ages 12-14*)

The topics identified here are not intended to exhaust the scope of sexuality education. Those listed focus only on the kind of factual information related to sexuality to be presented and explained. The child will:

1. learn how to deal with psycho-sexual changes, such as menstruation, wet dreams, sexual impulses, etc.
2. be given more detailed knowledge regarding the process of conception, fetal development, and birth.
3. understand the basic scientific facts and the Catholic teachings regarding birth control and contraception.
4. become familiar with psycho-sexual deviations such as homosexuality, transvestism, etc.

---

3. *Education in Human Sexuality*, p. 33.

5. explore in a Christian context some of the causes, effects, and myths related to masturbation.
6. become familiar with the more common venereal diseases, their causes, and their effects.
7. be given basic guidelines for responsible dating and for distinguishing authentic love from infatuation, physical attraction, seduction, etc.

## Summary

There are two major factors to consider in determining when your child should be taught certain aspects of human sexuality.

1. Intellectual and psychological readiness.
   Because children develop at a more or less predictable rate you can readily determine, at least in the general sense, what stage of development your child has achieved. The intellectual capacity and psychological maturity present are the keys to deciding what topics he or she can deal with effectively.
2. Experienced needs.
   The child's own growth will trigger the need to know certain kinds of information related to that growth. In addition, situations and circumstances can create "ad hoc" needs to learn more about particular topics.

In any event, it is good to keep in mind two underlying principles regarding when the child should receive sexuality education. First, sexuality education should be more or less continual throughout his or her developing years. Sexuality education is not limited to facts. It also embraces attitudes, religious values, moral behavior, and a full range of relational skills. Therefore, it remains an ongoing concern through each stage of the child's development.

Second, while we can predict in a general way the stages of each child's development, your child remains unique. As a parent, you are in the best position to recognize and appreciate your child's uniqueness. This gives you both the right and the responsibility to make the final decision regarding what you want your child to learn at any particular time.

This parent book and programs like the NEW CREATION program are intended to assist you. They are not intended to supplant your own good judgment regarding the sexuality education of your child.

# Chapter 4
# How to Approach Sexuality Education

## Introduction

This is usually the topic of most interest to parents, especially those who are dealing with sexuality education for the first time.

Sexuality education calls for delicacy and tact. It is not always an easy topic to talk about given the very personal nature of some aspects of the topic. It is natural enough, therefore, to look for help and practical suggestions.

We will share some of the wisdom that has been gained by concerned parents over the years, but there is one word of advice that should go before all the other suggestions. Do it *your* way. Trust your own instincts. Use your own strengths and admit your own limits. Do what seems right at the time for *your* child and what feels right to you, even if it seems to contradict some of the text book suggestions. Advice from others can be useful and may help you, but it is never intended to be followed blindly. Remember, *you* are the expert when it comes to dealing with your own child.

There is one other thought that most parents find consoling. It has to do with parenting in general, but it is especially appropriate in the area of sexuality education. You will make mistakes. You will mishandle particular situations; you will lose your patience on occasion; you will miss some good opportunities to guide and instruct your child; but it is extremely rare that a parent can make a particular mistake that will permanently harm a child.

It is the overall pattern of your parenting that you want to focus on, not particular situations. For example, if the general pattern of your communication with your child is good then the fact that you were a poor listener at some particular time should be viewed in that perspective. The good thing about parenting is that it lasts over a number of years. If the overall pattern of your parenting is good, the individual mistakes you are bound to make from time to time simply do not have the long range effect you sometimes fear they might. While this is true of parenting in general, it is especially true when educating your child about sexuality.

Now, let us consider some basic principles that are at work regarding how to communicate with your child in the area of sexuality. After that, we will focus on some specific issues most parents have to deal with at some time or another.

## Be Informed

This is the most fundamental need in terms of communicating with your child about sexuality. It will affect not only what you communicate, but it will in the final analysis determine how you communicate. Here are some areas you may want to review in regard to being informed.

**The Facts:** Do you have the facts about human sexuality and reproduction? You are not alone if you feel your own sexuality education was less than adequate. Most adults, especially in our sexually sophisticated times, find it very embarassing to admit that there are significant blank spaces in their knowledge about the parts of the human body or their precise role in the human reproductive system. No one is suggesting that you need to be an expert when it comes to the biological facts, but we do suggest that before you seek to discuss factual information with your child, you do your "homework." For the most part the kinds of information you will want to share with your child in the grade school years are quite basic. Doing your homework does not mean extensive review of medical books. The terms included in the glossary at the end of this book will usually be more than adequate. In addition, we have identified a number of books in the bibliography that present the factual information about human reproduction and the biology of the human body. Any one of them would be an adequate resource if you feel you need to brush up on some topic before you discuss it with your child.

In short, it is much better to admit to yourself that you need to do a little homework, than it would be to avoid certain issues because you are not sure of them. It would be even worse to pass on misinformation.

**Moral Convictions:** We have continually stressed that sexuality education includes imparting values and fostering moral convictions. In terms of knowing yourself, this means that you review just what it is you do believe. What are the values you are seeking to impart? What are your own moral convictions? Because of today's social climate in which many adults experience some doubts and confusion about what they believe, traditional values are being challenged. So it is important to determine what your own moral convictions are regarding such topics as masturbation; entertaining sexual fantasies; the morality of homosexuality; pornography; the importance of modesty in dress; divorce and remarriage; and the treatment of sexuality in movies, television, rock music, and advertising.

Because, either directly or indirectly, these are some of the moral issues that become involved in the sexuality education of your child, it is important that you seek to clarify your own position on such issues. Otherwise, you risk the danger of sending out mixed signals to your child, and in these formative years, the child needs clear guidelines and principles. Grade-school children are too young to be expected to work things out on their own. Therefore, know what your own position is before you try to discuss the topic with your child.

There is an important distinction to make in this regard. Certain kinds of behavior, that are all right for you as an adult, are inappropriate for your child. An obvious example is films or television fare suitable for adults but not for children. Typically, children have no trouble accepting such things. But you must guard against creating an artificial "double standard"—the "do as I say, not as I do" approach. You cannot view the Playboy channel on cable television, and, at the same time, expect to be credible when you try to teach that our sexuality deserves reverence and respect. In the area of sexuality, certain things are either right or wrong regardless of one's age. Be sure you know what items you want to present in that way. And then be prepared to model your convictions by your actions.

**Sexism:** Understanding the relationship between males and females and their roles in society and within the family is an integral part of sexuality education. As with various moral issues involving sexuality, this topic has a great deal of controversy surrounding it today. There have been some radical and far reaching changes in people's thinking in recent years. It is important that you know just what your own convictions and feelings on the topic are. It is those convictions and feelings, probably more than the words you use, that is likely to form your child's approach to the topic.

The Christian ideal is that men and women are of equal value in the eyes of God and that they deserve equal treatment and respect. Neither is intended by God or nature to be lower than or subservient to the other. Equal, of course, does not mean identical. There definitely are differences between males and females which we need to respect and protect.

What are those differences? That is something you have to clarify for yourself. If you are like most of us, you were exposed to many stereotyped ideas regarding those differences as you grew up. It would not be unusual if some forms of stereotyped thinking have become subconsciously ingrained, and unless you become aware of these stereotypes and correct them, you will unwittingly pass them on to your children. Because they may be ingrained, they are not always easy to recognize. They may be operating on a subconscious level and appear in subtle rather than obvious ways. You will want to work through this topic with your spouse and/or close friends of both sexes. They will be in the best position to help you recognize just what your convictions are, what you do feel, and what you communicate in this regard.

So know what you definitely want to communicate to your child and be in touch with what you are communicating. What your child comes to understand about the topic will have far-reaching effects on the rest of his or her life. Hopefully, what your child learns from you will be based on your conscious convictions, not unconscious misinformation you acquired in your own childhood.

**Personal Attitudes toward Sexuality:** We refer here to your own personal feelings toward yourself as a sexual person and toward sexuality in general. As with your attitudes toward the topic of sexism, your personal feelings about yourself and about sex are often acquired in subconscious ways and can operate at a subconscious level. Childhood experiences, your own parents' attitudes, what you were formally taught about sexuality in your formative years, your personal experience during the dating years, courtship, and marriage all have some influence on how you personally feel.

How can you evaluate yourself? Start by asking yourself the following questions regarding sexuality: Do you have an open, comfortable, positive attitude? Do you have mixed feelings? feelings of fear, aversion, guilt, embarrassment? negative feelings? How do you feel about your own body? about touching and being touched, physically expressing affection, having affection directed toward you? Are you comfortable with yourself as a sexual person? with your own sexual identity? with your sense of adequacy as a male or female person?

We are not suggesting you need to undergo psychoanalysis before you can undertake the sexuality education of your child, but it may call for a little soul-searching in order to get in touch with your real feelings. Nor are we suggesting that you can automatically change negative feelings or attitudes you may uncover. In some cases, these may be deeply rooted and virtually impossible to change. We are only suggesting that you be able to recognize or "name" your feelings and attitudes. By recognizing a particular unwanted fear or aversion in yourself, you can guard against passing it on to your child, even if you are unable to change it in yourself. If left unrecognized, there is a very good chance it will be acquired by your child in much the same way you acquired it.

Much of your child's sexuality education is going to be acquired in indirect ways by picking up your attitudes, feelings, values, and convictions in your everyday relationship with him or her. That is *how* you will be educating most of the time, and that is why it is so important that you strive to uncover your own most personal feelings and attitudes toward sexuality.

## Nonverbal Communication

Much of the "how" of sexuality education will take place in indirect ways. This indirect education is the nonverbal communication taking place in your relationship with your child.

Studies suggest that even in the earliest stages of infancy we communicate a great deal to the child simply in the way we handle him or her. These studies point out that something as simple as how we handle the baby when we are changing diapers can communicate something of our own feelings toward the body. This example may seem far-fetched to some, but the principle remains valid. We communicate a great deal to the growing child in nonverbal ways. It is good to be aware of several of the more important ways we do this.

**Affection:** How and when you express affection toward your spouse does not go unnoticed by the child. It can send a message that physical touch, hugging and kissing, embracing, and fondling are good and wholesome ways to express love. It can send a message that such acts are unnecessary or even unwholesome, that they should be guarded and secretive. The same is true in terms of how and when you express affection toward other adults of both sexes: your parents, relatives, close friends.

Most important of all, of course, is what you are communicating by the way you express affection toward the child. Everyone tends to agree today that the infant and very young child should receive a great deal of physical affection. It is also rather easy to express affection in a physical way toward babies and small children. But it is becoming more and more apparent that we long for and need the same kind of physical expressions of affection through all the formative years, during adulthood, and throughout old age. As body-persons we are designed to give and receive affection in embodied ways. Touch is our most universal sense. It is our most immediate contact with the world outside ourselves. It sends us many, deep messages about the nature of that world and about ourselves.

Therefore, modeling what you consider wholesome and appropriate ways of showing affection and exchanging physical expressions of affection with your child are two of your most important ways of communication about sexuality education.

Different cultures, ethnic groups, and individual families will have their own standards about what is appropriate and when it is appropriate. There is no universal standard that is best. You should go with what seems most natural to you. However, continue to ask yourself just what it is you are communicating to your child about his or her sexuality by the way you express physical affection. Then make sure that is what you really want to communicate.

**Modesty:** Each family tends to have its own standards regarding modesty within the home. Rules of modesty, regardless of what specific form they take, have two important roles to play in terms of sexuality education. They should promote a sense of the respect and privacy each person has a right to in regard to his or her own body. And they should nurture a sense of the goodness and naturalness of the human body, including its genital parts. Failing to guard your own right to privacy and failing to respect your child's right sends out one message, and an excessive concern about partial or total nudity, at times and in places when they are moral, sends out another message.

The key, then, is, first of all, determining what is a good balance within your own family and, second, promoting that standard not just by your words but more importantly by your actions and your reactions. You will be communicating a great deal about how your child should both respect and appreciate his or her body by the modesty you model and promote in your home.

Small children have a natural curiosity about the bodies of others, especially their siblings and parents. Overreacting to this can communicate the idea that there is something bad about the body. Older children, usually as they reach the middle grades if not sooner, begin quite naturally to develop a need for more privacy. While you may feel no embarrassment in seeing the child in a state of some undress or in you yourself appearing before the child in that way, it becomes important to respect the child's need. Only if there is an indication that the child's concern for modesty is excessive or morbid would you want to discuss it with the child.

Before considering other aspects of how to teach sexuality to your child, a general reminder may be appropriate regarding nonverbal communication. This kind of communication will go on all the time, even in instances where you are not present. The novels and magazines you have lying around the house can be telling your child something about your attitudes toward sexuality. The father who decorates his workroom with centerfold posters is saying something. Habits of personal neatness in dress and hygiene reflect the way you value your own body. You are constantly modeling your values and attitudes toward sexuality in your day-to-day behavior. Children, especially young children, absorb this modeling like sponges, in an uncritical way. They assume it is both normal and wholesome.

We want to stress the positive in saying this. You are probably doing much more wholesome educating in sexuality than you realize. Good example is every bit as powerful as bad example. At the same time, it is good to periodically review the kind of example you are manifesting through your day to day behavior.

## Verbal Communication

Some of the sexuality education you impart will be direct and intentional, verbal rather than nonverbal. In general, this kind of intentional verbal communication will take place in one of two settings. It will be initiated by you, either formally or informally. It will be initiated by the child through questions. We will look at some "how to's" for each of these settings shortly.

First, there are two principles to keep in mind in regard to all verbal communication with your child about sexuality:

- Use the correct words for the genitals and other parts of the body and for sexual functions. This is equally true for both the young and the older child. Young children take words literally. Telling the young child that "Mommie has a baby growing in her tummy" means for the child that the baby is in there with the mashed potatoes and meat loaf Mommie just ate for supper. Using "cute" words with younger children or slang words with older children—except to explain actual meaning—is never recommended.
- Be aware of your tone of voice, facial expressions, and body language (nonverbal elements of verbal communication) when you talk about sexuality. Children of any age are quick to pick up hints of nervousness, embarrassment, an angry or judgmental tone, etc. These may give a meaning to your words you do not wish to convey. If you do feel some embarrassment, it is better to simply say so. Tell your child you feel a little embarrassed talking about this because you never learned how to talk about it when you were young. Reinforce the fact that there is no need for embarrassment, nonetheless.

## Initiating Discussion

Parents often find it a challenge to know how and when to initiate some topic of sexuality they would like to discuss with the child. Sometimes, the problem is getting started. Sometimes the problem is getting the child to become involved instead of making it a monologue or a lecture. Setting the right tone can be a problem for some.

These seem to be rather common difficulties parents encounter. The following suggestions have proven helpful and you may want to try some of them.

**1. Take advantage of the NEW CREATION program.** Your child is participating in a formal program, and it provides many very natural opportunities to discuss specific topics with your child at each grade level. Home activities are suggested with each lesson. When helping your child do them, you have an opportunity to draw the child out by asking pertinent questions, and you also have the opportunity to make your own comments on the topic.

It is a real help if you do not always wait for the child to come to you. Anticipate home assignments. Ask the child what he or she wants you to do in regard to a particular lesson. Volunteer to help him or her study if a test or quiz is forthcoming. Your participation in the program on a regular basis can give you many natural opportunities to discuss matters of sexuality with your child. Equally important, it helps create a relationship where it is taken for granted that you can freely discuss sexuality together. Your child will feel free to approach you if the need arises. You will be able to take the initiative, at times, without it seeming like some extraordinary event. Your child's participation in the New Creation program during the grade school years can resolve most of the problems related to initiating discussions—provided you take an active part and show an active interest in the program.

**2. Take advantage of the circumstances.** A rock song with suggestive lyrics is playing on the car radio. You might ask a question like, "Is that guy saying what I think he's saying?" or "Do most kids agree with the ideas behind what he's singing?" Asking such questions is natural enough. Asking them in such a way that the child is not being personally accused of anything ("Is that guy. . . . ? Do most kids. . . ?) enables the child to give an objective response. Such an introduction can readily lead into a discussion about sexual values in society, your own values, and the child's ideas on the topic. The approach is informal and it takes advantage of the situation.

There are many such opportunities that you can either arrange ahead of time or respond to as they happen in day-to-day life. News stories on such events as the birth of a test tube baby, a rape, child abuse, an anti-abortion rally, an unusual multiple birth (quadruplets), a zoo's efforts to mate some rare species could all be used as an occasion to introduce a particular topic. Television shows and popular movies can present similar opportunities for initiating discussion. Stay alert for specials on television that focus on some sensitive topic. You may wish to arrange to view the show together with the express purpose of talking about it afterwards.

With smaller children, it is usually not as difficult to initiate discussion. They are less inhibited, tend to be candid, and have a wholesome, natural curiosity about life in general. However, there will be some "natural" times to initiate a conversation. A pregnancy or birth in the family is an obvious one, as is the birth of puppies or other pets. Trips to the zoo, the museum, and the library can be used effectively. Often, the child will take the initiative by raising questions spontaneously, but it is good to initiate a discussion as naturally and informally as possible whenever the occasion arises. This reinforces the idea that it is wholesome and good to talk to one another about sexuality.

**3. Arrange for a formal talk.** While it is good and usually sufficient to initiate a conversation as the opportunity arises, there will be occasions when you may want to sit down and have a serious talk. A few tips can help make this kind of talk come off as you intend it.

  a. **Give the child some warning and some sense of control over the situation.** A good approach is to say something to your child about his or her growing up so fast, and that you think it is time to have a good talk to be sure he or she knows what becoming a woman or man is really going to involve. Ask when it would be a good time for him or her.

  You have implied several things by doing this. You are taking it for granted that he or she already has some information, so the topic will not be totally new or threatening. You have also implied a lack of urgency. It does not have to be right now. It can be at the child's convenience. You are also giving the child some time to get mentally ready. All of this insures that the child will maintain some sense of control over the situation and hence be more open and responsive to what you do want to talk about.

b. **Choose a time and place which will be free of interruptions.** Children of any age can be easily distracted. Older children are likely to feel some self-consciousness. The risk of other people walking in on you can itself be a distraction to them. A phone call in the middle of the talk can break the mood and flow of thought. We do not want to give the impression that you should create a highly structured situation or a somber tone. The overall tone should be as informal and personable as possible, and as free as possible of interruptions.

c. **Let the child talk first.** It is good to begin by asking some simple, nonthreatening questions you are confident the child can answer. If there is any tension on the child's part, this will usually dispel it and bolster confidence. Proceed in this way, encouraging the child to tell you as much as he or she knows about the topic. This keeps the child involved, and it also keeps you from going over old ground which the child may find boring. Finally, it gives you a clue as to what you will need to add to the child's present knowledge. It is best not to interrupt. When the child has made his or her explanation, go back over it, affirming what was correct and adding anything that you want to add or correct.

By using this approach, you can avoid the trap of launching into some long talk while the child is forced to listen passively.

d. **Do not force questions from the child.** By all means, give ample opportunity for the child to ask you questions during such a session. But if none are forthcoming, do not keep encouraging them. It is quite possible the child either does not have any questions, or he or she is not quite ready to ask them.

e. **Do not drag it out.** The child's attention span is short. Interest wanes quickly. Before the session, decide precisely what points you hope to cover. As soon as you feel they are covered, terminate the session. Or as soon as the child, especially the younger child, shows signs of growing restless, terminate it even if you had hoped to cover more. Simply end by saying that there is more you would like to talk about but that you will get back to it later.

All this may sound like discussing sexuality with your child is complicated. It is not. That is why we keep suggesting that you follow your own instincts. Usually, they will tell you when it is the right time to initiate a conversation, how to pursue it, and when to end it.

## Answering Questions

When your child asks you a question related to sexuality, it is usually an excellent opportunity for the most effective sexuality education. The child is expressing an interest, which means he or she will be attentive to your answer, or the child is expressing a need, which means this may be the best time to deal with the topic raised. It also means the child already has a wholesome degree of openness about sexuality and has confidence in being able to talk about it with you.

If you keep the following principles in mind, you will answer questions effectively and you will continue to foster the child's openness and willingness to approach you in the future.

**1. Try not to overreact.** Sometimes, children can catch us totally off guard. The fact that the child has already heard about what he or she is asking may be a shock to you. If you show your shock, you put the child on the defensive, possibly awaken guilt, and certainly discourage the child from coming to you with other questions later.

**2. Take time to clarify the question.** It is important to be sure you understand what the child is asking. Does the child want a simple definition of a word, a more detailed explanation of how something works, or your opinion and advice on the morality of a specific form of sexual behavior? (Fact/Function/Morality)

You may discourage questions in the future if you give a lengthy explanation of the procreative process or the morality of nonmarital intercourse when the child only wants to know what the word "screwing" means simply because he or she heard other kids use it.

One good way to clarify is to redirect the question to the child by asking something safe like, "Do you have some idea of what it means?" or "What do you think it means?" or "I am not sure just what it is you want to know. Can you ask it another way?" or "What have you heard about it so far?" By getting a feel of just what is being asked and what the child already knows—or thinks he or she knows—you will be able to give a more direct, effective, and satisfying answer to the child.

In clarifying the nature of the question, avoid turning it into an investigation. Do not focus on questions like "Why would you ever want to know about that at your age?" or "Who have you been talking with?" or "Where did you hear about *that?*"

How the question occurred to the child is a secondary issue, if it is important at all. The child's desire to obtain information from you on a specific topic is what you want to address.

**3. It is all right to defer your answer.** You may not know the answer. If the topic is serious or complex, you may want to give it some thought before you answer. Simply explain that to the child while reassuring him or her that the question is a good one and you will answer it.

To defer is not the same as to put off, which is also a put-down for the child. It is definitely a put-off to suggest that the child is too young for information about a topic. Any question the child asks deserves some answer. You should tailor the amount of detail you present to the child's age and readiness, but you should always seek to give an effective answer.

**4. Be cautious in expanding on your answer.** This is related to the idea of clarifying the question. The question may focus on a fact, but could easily lend itself to exploring a moral issue, or could have other personal ramifications. For example, if your daughter asks how a girl knows when she is pregnant, she may simply want to know the mechanics of the pregnancy test she heard advertised on television, or she may be aware of a classmate or older girl who thinks she is pregnant.

Do not go into moral or other personal ramifications when that is not the child's concern even if the topic lends itself to doing so. Getting a lesson in morality when all that is wanted is a simple answer can discourage further questions. Timing is very important in introducing the moral implications of a topic. You do not need to use every question as an opportunity to reinforce the child's moral convictions.

## Dealing with Specific Issues

We have listed a few of the more common and often troublesome issues parents have to confront at some time or another during the grade-school years. The following suggestions may be helpful in developing your own approach to them.

**1. Obscene language:** First, take it for granted that your child will be exposed to it. Second, it is safe to presume that your child will probably experiment with using it, especially away from home and around peers. For your part, it is helpful to follow three rules:

   a. Never allow the child to use it in your presence.
   b. Stress that such language usually cheapens or reveals the ignorance of the user; is always in poor taste; usually offends and insults the hearers; and tends to cheapen and degrade human sexuality, which by its nature is good, beautiful, and holy. Rarely does obscene language used by children involve sinfulness, however, so this need not be stressed.
   c. Never use such language yourself, especially within the hearing of children, if you hope to discourage them from using it.

**2. Pornography:** This is something of an epidemic in most parts of the country. There is a good chance that your child will encounter it at some time or another. In seeking to help the child develop a proper understanding of its harmfulness, stress the following points:

   a. Pornography always degrades the persons involved, tends to reduce persons to "things," and often is produced by means of exploitation and violence directed toward women.

- b. Pornography always degrades human sexuality along with individual persons, making sexuality, which is good and beautiful, seem ugly, bad, and shameful.
- c. As a result, pornography tends to destroy respect for individual persons of both sexes and can seriously distort the viewer's understanding of and appreciation for his or her own sexuality.
- d. Pornography is not harmful in the fact by itself that it can cause sexual arousal and give sexual pleasure. Many good and wholesome things can have the same effect. The harmfulness of pornography should not be equated with sexual pleasure, but with the appropriateness of sexual pleasure at that time and place and in those conditions and also of what is causing that pleasure: the degradation of persons and of human sexuality. Children should be taught when and to what degree sexual pleasure is appropriate. And we should never want to seek personal pleasure by means of degrading or using other persons as if they were objects.

**3. Monitoring television and movies:** From the child's earliest years onward, he or she will be exposed to sexual values and specific forms of sexual behavior presented in the media. Some of it will be counter to your own values. Some of it may be too explicit or too advanced for the child. To minimize this unwanted exposure (you cannot hope to totally eliminate it), the following suggestions may be helpful:

- a. Begin in the earliest years to set certain time limits on how much television the child can watch and what programs are allowed. The very young child will usually accept these limits without challenge. By starting early in childhood, you are establishing the principle that in your family it is normal to have limits on viewing television. Then, as the child gets older, it is possible to continue a practice that is taken for granted. You can expand and adapt the limits, but you do not have to defend the principle of setting limits.
- b. Do the same in terms of attending movies. Set limits regarding how often and what kind of movies the child can attend. Follow through as the child gets older, making necessary adjustments.

c. When you find it necessary to forbid the older child some movie, TV show, or rock concert, even though "all the other kids are going," be as creative as possible in suggesting or providing an alternative which has some appeal to the child, e.g., allow the child to have some friends over for a party, or suggest a family outing.

   The alternative may never have the same appeal as what the child originally wanted to do, but it is usually more effective than the "No" unaccompanied by an alternative.
d. Sometimes, it is useful to attend a questionable film with the child and follow it with a discussion of the child's impressions and your own about the merits and offensiveness of it.
e. In seeking to explain why you are opposed to certain TV programs, movies, and other forms of entertainment, the objections to pornography mentioned above can be helpful, because the same principles often are involved, though to a lesser degree.

## Summary

After reading this chapter, you are aware that what is involved in sexuality education involves the principles of good parenting in general.

We need to know ourselves, our thoughts, our feelings, and our convictions in order to communicate them effectively to our children. This communication is both verbal and nonverbal.

Effective sexuality education does not require complex methods, special training, or special expertise. It requires common sense and personal concern.

By reviewing this chapter, you should be encouraged, because you have probably noted that you are already doing much of what is being suggested. Some suggestions will not apply to your situation, but hopefully you have discovered, or been reminded of, some things that you had not related to sexuality education and parenting.

Be confident that your own efforts, complemented and reinforced by your child's participation in the NEW CREATION program, are providing the sexuality education you want your child to have.

# Appendix I

## Summaries of Selected Moral Issues

Five of the more significant and controversial moral issues are summarized below. Summaries include a brief explanation of the areas of debate and the Church's official position on the subject.

They are intended primarily for background reading. You may want to refer to them before the topics come up in discussion with your child.

## Issue: Artificial Means of Achieving Pregnancy

1. **Definition**
   a. Artificial insemination: implanting semen within the woman by medical intervention rather than intercourse. The fertilization of an ovum, however, takes place within the woman's body in the way sperm and ovum would ordinarily unite after intercourse. Sometimes the semen is from the husband, sometimes from a sperm bank or another donor.
   b. Fertilization in vitro ("test-tube" baby): removing an ovum from the woman's body and fertilizing it with a donor's sperm in a laboratory; then medically implanting the fertilized ovum within the woman with the hope that it will grow to full term.
2. **Areas of Debate**
   a. Modern medicine is an outgrowth of human potential. If it can be done and if it does great good, it can be justified.
   b. The end can justify the means in this instance; the Church's natural law approach to human sexuality is outdated.

3. **Church Position**
   The Church considers such practices sinful in principle, objectively immoral. The sinfulness is compounded when donor and recipient are not married.

4. **Rationale**
   a. Although the intentions may be noble, such actions interfere with the purposes of marriage and of human sexuality and they violate human dignity. It is a case of the ends not justifying the means.
   b. When male donor and female recipient are not married the fidelity principle of marriage is objectively violated.
   c. The recent potential for surrogate motherhood (a fertilized ovum from a woman is implanted in another woman) is challenged on the same principle interfering with both the sacredness of marriage and the human and natural processes of human sexuality.
   d. Many ova fertilized in vitro die before being successfully transplanted. Such fertilized ova are human beings. Such "experimenting" with human life is abhorrent in the context of the fifth commandment and the dignity of persons.

# Issue: Masturbation (Autoeroticism)

1. **Definition**
   Stimulating one's own genitals manually or in other ways to achieve orgasm.

2. **Areas of Debate**
   a. Questions have been raised about whether masturbation is a grave matter, and pastoral theologians stress that, while masturbation is sinful in principle, extenuating circumstances may minimize or completely eradicate personal guilt. They apply this especially to adolescents.
   b. Masturbation may be symptomatic of a more serious disorder, including a personality dysfunction in some instances. Attention should be placed less on the act than on the causes for the act.

c. Secular humanist psychologists argue that masturbation is a normal and healthy stage of sexual development for adolescents and should not be discouraged.

**3. Church Position**
This is considered seriously sinful in principle.

**4. Rationale**
Genital sexual expressions are intended to be open to life and unitive. Masturbation contradicts both these purposes and is therefore a disordered expression of genital sexuality. It is tainted by selfishness by its very nature.

Statement on Autoeroticism taken from *Educational Guidance in Human Love* (Vatican Statement on Sexuality).

**(Autoeroticism)** *It is the task of sex education to promote a continuous progress in the control of the impulses to effect an opening, in due course, to true and self-giving love. A particularly complex and delicate problem which can be present is that of masturbation and of its repercussions on the integral growth of the person. Masturbation, according to catholic doctrine, constitutes a grave moral disorder principally because it is the use of sexual faculty in a way which essentially contradicts its finality, not being at the service of love and life according to the design of God.*

**(Causes)** *A teacher and perspicacious counselor must endeavor to identify the causes of the deviation in order to help the adolescent to overcome the immaturity underlying this habit. From an educative point of view, it is necessary to consider masturbation and other forms of autoeroticism as symptoms of problems much more profound, which provoke sexual tension which the individual seeks to resolve by recourse to such behavior. Pedagogic action, therefore, should be directed more to the causes than to the direct repression of the phenomenon.*

*Whilst taking account of the objective gravity of masturbation, it is necessary to be cautious in evaluating the subjective responsibility of the person.*

**(Help against Autoeroticism)** *In order that the adolescent be helped to feel accepted in a communion of charity and freed from self-enclosure, the teacher "should undramatise masturbation and not reduce his or her esteem and benevolence for the pupil." The teacher will help the pupil toward social integration, to be open and interested in others, to be able to be free from this form of autoeroticism, advancing toward self-giving love, proper to mature affectivity; at the same time, the teacher will encourage the pupil to have recourse to the recommended means of Christian asceticism, such as prayer and the sacraments, and to be involved in works of justice and charity.*

## Issue: Artificial Birth Control Methods

1. **Definition**
   a. Any mechanical (condom, IUD, diaphragm) or chemical (pill, foams) intervention intended to prevent the fertilization of an ovum by a sperm. Also called contraceptives.
   b. Any nontherapeutic surgical intervention for the same purpose (vasectomy, tubal ligation).
2. **Areas of Debate**
   a. Some argue that the capacity of the human intelligence to develop methods to avoid pregnancies while still engaging in marital intercourse makes those forms of birth control moral, provided the motives for avoiding or limiting conceptions are unselfish and life-oriented. The argument is that the mind is natural and its intentionalities and creations can be natural and moral even if physical nature is altered.
   b. Some challenge the underlying natural law approach to morality—and specifically to—intercourse upon which the Church's position is based.
3. **Church Position**
   Any artificial or nonnatural method used to prevent conception is gravely sinful in principle. Natural methods, such as periodic abstinence, the sympto-thermal method, and natural family planning approaches are allowed, provided the couple's decision to

limit or regulate conceptions is based on unselfish, life-oriented, and loving motives.

4. **Rationale**

Sexual intercourse is ordained by God to be love-giving and to be life-giving, both literally in terms of possible conception and spiritually in terms of expressing and enhancing the spiritual union of the couple.

It is therefore morally wrong to redirect God's intended love-giving and life-giving purposes for sexual intercourse by artificial interventions to prevent conception or to reduce intercourse to a form of self-indulgence irrespective of its meaning and effect for the marriage relationship.

# Issue: Abortion

1. **Definition**
   a. Volitional abortion: surgical or other intervention intended to destroy and/or remove from the woman's body a fertilized, living ovum at any stage in its development; zygote, embryo, or fetus.
   b. Involuntary, natural or spontaneous abortion (miscarriage): the expulsion from a woman's body of a fertilized ovum at any stage in its development after it has already died or before it can be sustained and continue in its development outside the womb.

2. **Areas of Debate**
   a. The highest priority is given to the pregnant woman's choice by pro-abortionists.
   b. The vast majority of pro-abortion advocates consider the fertilized ovum either not to be a human being or else not to have the right to life until it has reached some specific stage in its development. Pro-abortionists do not agree on the stage at which the "growth" within the mother becomes a human being with the right to life. Often times, these questions will not even be discussed on the grounds that it is the woman's choice which has priority always.
   c. Some seek to expand the concept of a "life-threatening" condition on the part of the woman to include more intangible aspects such as emotional or

mental health, or the impact on the woman's relationship to her spouse and/or children. This principle is often argued in cases of pregnancy due to rape or incest, especially if the pregnant female is still in her teens.
   d. Some seek to justify abortion in instances where serious birth defects—mental or physical—can be anticipated if the fetus is allowed to develop to term.
3. **Church Position**
Volitional abortion is always gravely sinful and an "unspeakable crime" except in those cases where the abortion is a possible or necessary, but not directly intended, result of efforts to treat the mother for a life-threatening illness and no alternative treatment is possible. Ectopic pregnancy is the clearest example. The fetus is removed even though its unintended death will follow.
4. **Rationale**
The Church's position is based on the conviction that a new human being with an immortal soul, loved and created by God, comes into existence at the moment of the union of an ovum and sperm. As such, the fertilized, living ovum at any stage in its development has all the rights endowed on all human beings, the most basic being the right to life.

# Issue: Homosexuality

1. **Definition**
   a. The state or condition by which a person's basic attraction is toward persons of the same sex and a lack of sexual attraction (or actual aversion) for persons of the opposite sex.
   b. Genital sexual acts performed with a person of the same sex.
2. **Areas of Debate**
   a. Some argue that those who are homosexual through no fault of their own and unable to change this condition should be allowed sexual expression of love within committed relationships as a lesser of two evils or a compromise in a less than perfect world.
   b. Some argue that homosexuality is the natural state

for some individuals even though heterosexuality is the natural state for the majority of humans. Therefore, genital expressions of love between homosexuals in a committed relationship is natural for them.

Advocates of this position maintain that Scriptures are not always properly understood in reference to homosexuality. They are described as perversions for heterosexuals who engage in them and must be read in that context.

3. **Church Position**
   a. The state or condition of homosexuality is not considered sinful as such. Causes for this condition vary. The individual may or may not be responsible for or capable of changing the orientation. No general judgment can be passed that can be applied to all persons in this state.
   b. *All* genital sexual acts outside of marriage are sinful, including gential sexual acts performed between persons of the same sex.

4. **Rationale**
   a. Marriage is not allowed by the Church or state between persons of the same sex. All genital sexual acts between persons of the same sex must necessarily take place outside of wedlock and are therefore sinful.
   b. Genital sexual acts are intended to be open to the procreation of life. Genital sexual acts between homosexuals cannot fulfill this human and natural purpose of sex and are therefore sinful.
   c. Scripture identifies homosexual/sexual acts (male or female) as perversions. A pastoral approach which is both challenging and comforting is recommended here just as much as in other types of cases.

# Further Reading

Avento, Fr., C.P. *Sexuality, A Christian View*, Twenty Third Publications, Mystic, CT

Curran, Charles. *Issues in Sexual and Medical Ethics*, University of Notre Dame, Press, Notre Dame, IN

*Educational Guidance in Human Love.* Vatican Statement on Sexuality.

Grisez, Germain. *Contraception and the Natural Law,* Bruce, Milwaukee.

———. *Abortion: Myths, the Realities and the Arguments.*

Haughton, Rosemary. *The Holiness of Sex,* Abbey Press, St. Meinrad, IN

Keane, Fr. Philip. *Sexual Morality: A Catholic Perspective,* Paulist Press, Ramsey, NJ
Fr. Philip Keane's book is a good source for finding out the various positions of theologians today, but is not intended to and does not reflect official Catholic doctrine on every issue. For this reason and because it did not technically require an *imprimatur* under the code of Cannon Law issued after the book, the imprimatur on this book was withdrawn.

Kennedy, Eugene. *What a Modern Catholic Believes about Sex,* The St. Thomas More Press, Chicago, IL

Mackin, Theodore. *Divorce and Remarriage,* Paulist Press, Ramsey, NJ

———. *What Is Marriage?* Paulist Press, Ramsey, NJ

May, William and Harvey, John. *On Understanding Human Sexuality,* Franciscan Herald Press, Chicago.

National Conference of Catholic Bishops. Pastoral letter, *Human Life in Our Day* November, 1968.

On Moral Values in Society. NCCB Ad Hoc Committee on Moral Values, November 1974.

On the Family, Apostolic Exhortation *Familiaris Consortio,* December 15, 1981.

On the Regulation of Birth (*Humanae Vitae*). Encyclical, Pope Paul VI, July 25, 1968.

Pastoral Constitution on the Church in the Modern World (*Gaudium et Spes*). The Pope and bishops at Vatican II.

Pastoral letter of Bishop Francis Mugavero. *Sexuality—God's Gifts,* St. Anthony Messenger Press, 1615 Republic Street, Cincinnati, OH 45310

# Appendix II

## Glossary

The following glossary is used in the NEW CREATION program. It is intended for both parents and teachers. Edited versions are included in the student texts for the upper-grade levels, adapted to their needs and readiness.

**Abortion (a-BOR-shun)** The termination of a pregnancy before birth would be expected. There are three types:
*voluntary*, the deliberate expulsion and/or killing of the embryo or fetus by the decision;
*spontaneous* (miscarriage), a natural termination usually due to some abnormal development of the embryo or fetus;
*therapeutic*, abortion based on the grounds that the pregnancy threatens the mother's life. Sometimes this term is also used to mean abortion of a genetically defective fetus or an abortion performed because the pregnancy is considered a threat to the health, not the life, of the pregnant woman.

**Abstinence (AB-stin-ens)** To voluntarily avoid: In sexual connotation, to refrain from sexual intercourse.

**Acne (AK-nee)** A condition of the complexion characterized by pimples, blackheads, and/or excess oiliness. Common in adolescents.

**Adolescence (a-doh-LES-sens)** The period of life between puberty and adulthood.

**Adultery (a-DULL-ter-ee)** Sexual intercourse by a person who is legally married with someone other than one's mate. The term is sometimes used to describe any sexual intercourse outside marriage.

**Amniocentesis (am-nee-o-sen-TEE-sis)** A procedure whereby a sample of the amniotic fluid surrounding the fetus is drawn and analyzed to detect possible birth defects or the sex of the fetus. Damages or kills the fetus in a small percent of cases.

**Amnion (AM-nee-on)**   The thin membrane which forms the sac of water surrounding the fetus within the uterus. Contains amniotic fluid in which the fetus is immersed for protection against shocks and jolts.

**Androgen (AN-dro-jen)**   A male hormone which influences growth and the sex drive. Produces masculine secondary sex characteristics (voice changes, hair growth, etc.)

**Anus (AY-nus)**   The opening at the base of the buttocks through which solid waste is eliminated from the intestines.

**Artificial Insemination**   The medical procedure of injecting semen—from the husband, from a sperm bank, or from another donor—into the vagina close to the cervix by artificial means; can enable pregnancy in spite of fertility problems.

**Birth Control**   See contraception.

**Bisexual (by-SECKS-shoo-al)**   Term commonly used to describe a sexual interest in both sexes.

**Bladder (BLAD-er)**   A sac in the pelvic region where urine is stored until elimination.

**Breech Birth**   The birth position when the baby's feet or buttocks appear first instead of the usual (head first) position.

**Caesarean Section (si-SAIR-ee-an)**   Delivery of a baby by surgical incision through the abdomen into the uterus. Also called caesarean birth and "C" section.

**Castration (kas-TRAY-shun)**   Removal of the sex glands—the testicles in men, the ovaries in women.

**Cervix (SER-vicks)**   The narrow, lower part of the uterus, which opens into the deep portion of the vagina.

**Chancre (SHANG-ker)**   A small sore or ulcerated area, usually on the genitals, which is the first symptom of syphillis.

**Chastity (CHAS-ti-tee)**   Positively, the virtue by which a person respects and properly expresses his or her sexuality. Negatively, abstention from illicit sexual intercourse.

**Chromosome (KRO-mo-soam)** One of the rodlike bodies found in the nucleus of all cells, containing the heredity factors or genes. Twenty-two pairs of chromosomes account for a person's hereditary characteristics. The twenty-third pair determines sex. See X Chromosome and Y Chromosome.

**Circumcision (ser-kum-SIZH-un)** Surgical removal of the foreskin or prepuce of the penis. Originally, a Jewish rite performed as a sign of reception into their faith; now generally performed for purposes of cleanliness. No longer automatically recommended by doctors.

**Climacteric (kly-MACK-ter-ik)** The time of physical and emotional change—end of menstruation in women and lessening of sex-hormone production in both sexes. See Menopause and Mid-life Crisis

**Climax** See orgasm.

**Clitoris (KLIT-or-iss)** A small, highly sensitive female organ located just above the urethra. Compares to the penis in males.

**Coitus (KO-ih-tus)** Sexual intercourse between male and female, in which the penis is inserted into the vagina.

**Conception (kon-SEP-shun)** (Impregnation) Penetration of the ovum (female egg cell) by a sperm, resulting in development of an embryo—new life.

**Condom** See Contraception

**Congenital (kon-JEN-i-tal)** Any condition existing from birth which is not genetic or inherited, e.g., congenital blindness from damage that occurs in birth. (Literally "with birth" **not** "with genes," but the nongenetic condition could develop **before** birth.).

**Contraception (kon-trah-SEP-shun)** (Birth Control) The prevention of conception by use of devices, drugs, or other means before or during sexual intercourse. Commonly used methods are:
*Birth Control Pill* A contraceptive drug made of synthetic hormones which prevents ovulation or in some cases causes the expulsion of a fertilized ovum (e.g., morning after pill). Available only by prescription and must be taken as prescribed. There can be negative side-effects, including death.

*Condom* (KON-dum) A thin rubber sheath placed over the erect penis before intercourse to prevent the sperm from entering the vagina.

*Vaginal Foam, Jelly, Suppositories, etc.* Nonprescription products for the female which are applied within the vagina. Most contain a spermicide—chemical substance which destroys sperm cells.

*Diaphragm* (DIE-a-fram) A thin rubber disc which covers the cervix and prevents sperm from entering the uterus. Must be individually fitted by a doctor.

*Premature Withdrawal* Withdrawal of the penis from the vagina before ejaculation. Unreliable because of possible release of sperm before ejaculation.

*Rhythm Method* Abstinence from intercourse during the woman's fertile days as determined by her menstrual cycle. A method based on a calendar recording of a woman's menstrual periods.

*Natural Family Planning* Abstinence from intercourse during a woman's fertile days. It is a method based on body temperature changes and/or the consistency of the cervical mucus during fertility.

**Copulation**  See coitus

**D & C**  (*Dilatation & Curettage*) A medical procedure in which the cervix is dilated and a spoon-shaped medical instrument called a curette is used to scrape the lining of the uterus. It is used for abortion up to the twelfth week.

**Delivery**  The process of giving birth.

**Douche (doosh)**  The cleansing of the vagina with a stream of liquid solution or water. Medically, it is debatable whether or not it is necessary.

**Ejaculation (ee-jack-yoo-LAY-shun)**  The discharge of semen from the penis.

**Embryo (EM-bree-oh)**  The unborn in its earliest stages of development. In humans, the fertilized ovum during the first eight weeks of its growth.

**Endometrium (en-doh-MEE-tree-um)**  The lining of the uterus, which thickens and fills with blood in preparation for a fertilized ovum.

**Epididymis (ee-pi-DID-i-miss)**  The mass of tiny coils connecting the testicles with the sperm duct.

**Erection (ee-RECK-shun)** The enlargement and hardening of the penis or clitoris as tissues fill with blood, usually during sexual excitement.

**Erogenous Zone (ee-RAH-jen-us)** Any area of the body that is sexually sensitive or stimulating such as mouth, lips, breasts, nipples, and genitals.

**Erotic (ee-RAH-tik)** Sexually stimulating

**Estrogen (ESS-tro-jen)** A female hormone which affects functioning of the menstrual cycle and produces female secondary sex characteristics (breast development, widened hips, etc.)

**Eunuch (YOO-nuck)** A castrated male.

**Exhibitionist (ex-i-BISH-un-ist)** A person who compulsively exposes his or her sex organs in public.

**Extramarital (ex-tra-MARE-i-tal)** Outside of marriage; often used to refer to illicit sexual intercourse (extramarital affair).

**Fallopian Tube (fa-LOW-pee-an)** The tube through which the egg passes from each ovary to the uterus.

**Fertility** The ability to reproduce.

**Fertilization** Penetration of the female ovum by a single sperm, resulting in conception.

**Fetus (FEE-tuss)** The unborn child from the third month after conception until after birth.

**Foreplay** The beginning stage of sexual intercourse, during which partners may kiss, caress, and touch each other with intimate actions in order to achieve full sexual arousal.

**Foreskin** The loose skin covering the tip of the penis, removed during circumcision. Also called the prepuce (PREE-puce). This procedure is no longer automatically recommended.

**Fornication (for-ni-Kay-shun)** Sexual intercourse between unmarried men and women.

**Frigidity (fri-JID-i-tee)** Term commonly used, sometimes unfairly and cruelly, for the sexual dysfunction in which a woman is unable to respond to sexual stimulation.

**Gene (jean)** The carrier for hereditary traits in chromosomes.

**Genital Herpes** See venereal disease

**Genitalia (jen-i-TAIL-ya)** (Genitals; Genital Organs) Visible reproductive or sex organs. Usually denotes vagina, vulva, and clitoris in females and the penis and testicles in males.

**Gestation (jes-TAY-shun)** The period from conception to birth, approximately nine months.

**Glans (glanz)** The head of the penis, exposed either when the foreskin is pushed back or permanently after circumcision.

**Gonorrhea (gon-er-EE-uh)** See venereal disease

**Gynecologist (guy-na-KOLL-o-jist)** A physician who specializes in treatment of female sexual and reproductive organs and their functions.

**Heredity (her-ED-it-ee)** Traits, characteristics, or diseases transmitted from parents to children.

**Heterosexual (het-er-o-SECK-shoo-al)** One who is sexually attracted to or sexually active with persons of the other sex.

**Homosexual (ho-mo-SECK-shoo-al)** One who is sexually attracted to or sexually active with persons of one's own sex.

**Hormone (HOR-moan)** A chemical substance, produced by an endocrine gland, which has a particular effect on the function of organs in the body.

**Hymen (HIGH-men)** A thin membrane which partially closes the entrance to the vagina. Sometimes called the maidenhead.

**Hysterectomy (hiss-ter-ECK-to-mee)** Surgical removal of the uterus. May include removal of one or both ovaries (oophorectomy).

**Impotence (IM-po-tens)** A type of male sexual dysfunction; inability to achieve or maintain erection of the penis during sexual intercourse.

**Incest (IN-sest)**   Sexual intercourse between close relatives such as father and daughter, mother and son, or brother and sister.

**Intercourse (Sexual)**   See coitus.

**Jock Itch**   A fungus infection causing skin irritation in the genital area.

**Labor**   The birth stage in which the cervix gradually dilates, allowing strong contractions of the uterine muscles to push the baby through the vagina and out of the mother's body.

**Lactation (lak-TAY-shun)**   The production and secretion of milk by the mammary glands in the mother's breasts, following childbirth. The process continues so long as she nurses her child.

**Lesbian (LEZ-be-an)**   A female homosexual.

**Libido**   See sex drive

**Maidenhead**   See hymen

**Masturbation (mass-ter-BAY-shun)**   Self-stimulation of one's sex organs, often to the point of orgasm.

**Menarche (me-NAR-kee)**   The onset of the menstrual cycle in a girl.

**Menopause (MEN-o-pawz)**   (Change of Life; Climacteric) The end of menstruation in women, usually between the ages of forty-five and fifty-five.

**Menstruation (men-stroo-AY-shun)**   The discharge through the vagina of blood from the uterus. This menstrual "period" usually occurs every twenty-eight to thirty days in females between puberty and menopause. But there can be a wide variance in that number even in the same woman from month to month.

**Mid-life Crisis**   Current term for the change of life (climacteric) in men, usually between ages fifty and sixty; sometimes called male menopause. May evoke feelings of restlessness and failure, including sexual feelings of failure or restlessness.

**Miscarriage**   (Spontaneous Abortion) The natural expulsion of the embryo or fetus from the uterus before it is mature enough to live outside the womb, usually due to some abnormal development.

**Nocturnal Emission (nok-TER-nal-ee-MISH-un)** (Wet Dream) Involuntary male erection and ejaculation during sleep.

**Obstetrician (ob-ste-TRISH-un)** A physician who specializes in the care of women during pregnancy, childbirth, and immediately thereafter.

**Orgasm (OR-gazm)** (Climax) The peak of excitement in sexual activity.

**Ovaries (OH-va-rees)** The two female sex glands found on either side of the uterus, in which the ova (egg cells) are formed. They also produce hormones which influence female body characteristics.

**Ovulation (oh-vyoo-LAY-shun)** Release of the mature (ripe) ovum from the ovary to one of the fallopian tubes.

**Ovum (OH-vum)** (Plural: ova) Female reproductive cell (egg) found in the ovary. After fertilization by a male sperm, the human zygote or fertilized egg develops into an embryo and then a fetus.

**Penis (PEE-nis)** Male sex organ through which semen is discharged and urine is passed.

**Pituitary (pih-TOO-it-air-ee)** A gland at the base of the brain which controls functions of all the other ductless glands, especially sex glands, adrenals, and thyroid.

**Placenta (pla-SEN-ta)** The sponge-like organ that connects the fetus to the lining of the uterus by means of the umbilical cord. It serves to feed the fetus and to dispose of waste. Expelled from the uterus after the birth of a child (afterbirth).

**Pornography (por-NOG-raf-ee)** Literature, motion pictures, art, or other means of expression which, without any concern for moral values or the values of persons, intend simply to be sexually arousing.

**Pregnancy (PREG-nan-cee)** Period from conception to birth; the presence of a developing embryo or fetus within the female body.

**Prenatal (pree-NAY-tal)** Before birth.

**Progesterone (pro-JES-ter-own)** (Progestin) The female "pregnancy hormone" which prepares the uterus to receive the fertilized ovum.

**Promiscuous (pro-MISS-kyoo-us)** Engaging in sexual intercourse with multiple persons and without commitment; engaging in casual sexual relationships.

**Prophylactic (prah-fil-LAK-tik)** A device or drug used to prevent disease, often specifically venereal disease. Common term for the condom.

**Prostate (PRAH-state)** Male gland which surrounds the urethra and neck of the bladder and secretes part of the seminal fluid.

**Prostitute (PRAH-sti-toot)** An individual who engages in sexual activity for money.

**Puberty (PYOO-ber-tee)** The period of rapid development that marks the end of childhood; sex organs mature and produce either ovaries or sperm; the girl becomes a young woman and the boy a young man.

**Pubic (PYOO-bik)** Regarding the lower part of the abdominal area, where hair grows in a triangular patch.

**Rape (rayp)** Forcible sexual intercourse with a person who does not consent. *Statutory rape* means having intercourse with a consenting minor who is under the legal age for intercourse in that state.

**Rectum (RECK-tum)** The lower end of the large intestine, ending at the anus.

**Rhythm Method** See contraception

**Safe Period** The interval in the menstrual cycle when the female is presumably not ovulating and therefore unable to become pregnant.

**Scrotum (SKRO-tum)** The sac of skin suspended between the male's legs that contains the testicles.

**Semen (SEE-men)** (Seminal Fluid; Seminal Emmission) The fluid made up of sperm, secretions from the seminal vesicles, prostate and Cowper's glands, and the epididymis. Ejaculated through the penis when the male reaches orgasm.

**Seminal Vesicles (SEM-i-nal VESS-i-cals)** Two storage pouches for sperm (which is produced in the testicles). Located on either side of the prostate, they are attached to and open into the sperm ducts.

**Sex Drive**   (Libido: li-BEE-doe) The desire for sexual activity.

**Sex Organs**   Commonly refers to the male penis and female vagina.

**Sexual Dysfunction**   Term used to describe problems in sexual performance.

**Sexual Intercourse**   See coitus

**Sodomy (SAH-dah-mee)**   Any of a variety of sexual behaviors, broadly defined by law as deviant, such as sexual intercourse by humans of the same sex, especially males by anal intercourse, or intercourse by mouth-genital contact, or intercourse with animals.

**Sperm**   The male reproductive cell(s), produced in the testicles, having the capacity to fertilize the female ovum, resulting in pregnancy.

**Spermatic Duct (sper-MAT-ik)**   (Vas Deferens) The tube in the male through which sperm passes from the epididymis to the seminal vesicles and urethra.

**Spermatic Cord**   The tube in the male by which the testicle is suspended; contains the sperm ducts, veins, and nerves.

**Spermicide**   See contraception

**Spontaneous Abortion**   See miscarriage

**Sterility (ster-ILL-it-ee)**   The inability to reproduce.

**Sterilization (ster-ill-ih-ZAY-shun)**   A procedure by which a male or female is rendered unable to produce children, but can still engage in sexual intercourse. Some of the most common surgical methods are:
*Laparoscopy* (la-pa-ROS-ko-pee) Tiny incisions in the abdomen, through which the fallopian tubes are cut or cauterized. Also called "Band-Aid Sterilization."
*Tubal Ligation* (TOO-bul lie-GAY-shun) The surgeon cuts and ties the ends of both fallopian tubes after making a larger incision in the abdomen or by going through the vagina.
*Vasectomy* (vas-ECK-toe-mee) The male sperm-carrying duct is cut, part is removed, and the ends are tied.

**Syphilis**   See venereal disease

**Testes (TES-teez)** (Testicles) The two male sex glands which produce sperm; suspended within a sac of skin between the legs.

**Testosterone (tes-TOSS-ter-own)** Male sex hormone produced by the testes; causes and maintains male secondary sex characteristics (voice change, hair growth, etc.)

**Transgenderist (trans-JEN-der-ist)** A person who identifies very strongly with the other sex and may dress in clothing of that sex.

**Transsexual (trans-SEKS-shoo-al)** One who feels psychologically like a member of the other sex, and perhaps even undergos "sex change" surgery to achieve the outward appearance of the other sex.

**Transvestite** One who has a compulsion to dress in clothing of the other sex.

**Trichomoniasis (trick-uh-muh-NY-us-sis)** See veneral disease

**Umbilical Cord (uhm-BILL-ih-kal)** The cord connecting the fetus to the placenta, through which the fetus receives nourishment and waste is removed.

**Urethra (yoo-REE-thra)** The duct through which urine passes from the bladder and is eliminated from the body.

**Urologist (yoo-RAHL-i-jist)** A physician who specializes in treating urinary tract problems of both sexes, as well as the genital tract of males.

**Uterus (YOO-ter-us)** (Womb: woom) The small, muscular, pear-shaped female organ in which the fetus develops; has the ability to expand to accommodate the growing child (children).

**Vagina (vuh-JY-na)** (Birth Canal) The canal in the female body between the uterus and the vulva; receives the penis during intercourse; the canal through which an infant passes at birth.

**Vasectomy** See sterilization

**Venereal Disease (ven-NEAR-ee-al)** (VD) Any of a variety of contagious diseases contracted almost entirely by sexual intercourse. Some of the most common are: Genital Herpes; Gonorrhea; Syphilis.

**Virgin (VER-jin)**   A person who has never had sexual intercourse.

**Vulva (VUL-va)**   The female's external sex organs, including the Labia majora and Labia minora, the outer and inner folds of skin (lips) surrounding the vagina and the clitoris.

**Wasserman Test**   A blood test to determine present or past infection with syphilis.

**Wet Dream**   See nocturnal emission

**Womb**   See uterus

**X Chromosome**   A chromosome which determines gender, present in all female ova and in one-half of a male's sperm. If the egg is fertilized by a sperm having an X chromosome, a female will be conceived (XX).

**Y Chromosome**   A sex-determining chromosome present in one-half of a male's sperm. If an ovum is fertilized by a sperm with a Y chromosome, a male will be conceived (XY).

**Zygote (ZY-goat)**   The fertilized egg.

# Appendix III

## Anatomical Illustrations Related to the Reproductive System

The following are intended only as a quick refresher should you need to review the anatomy of the male and female reproductive systems, the menstrual cycle, and the conception process.

For more detailed information, you may want to consult one of the following books which are available at your public library:

Bengly, D. J. *Human Reproduction and Development Biology*, Macmillan, New York

Carnation Company. *Pregnancy in Anatomical Illustrations*, Los Angeles, CA

Diagram Group. *Man's Body*, Paddington Press, New York\*

————. *Woman's Body*, Paddington Press, New York\*

Haberle, Erwin. *The Sex Atlas*, Seabury Press, New York

Nilsson, Lennart, *A Child Is Born*, Delacorte Press, New York

Pansky, B. *Dynamic Anatomy and Physiology*, Macmillan Publishers, New York

\*Excellent factual information. Not recommended as a source on ethical issues.

# Male Genital System

Major parts of the male genital system are shown together with the area around them, mainly those parts involved in the elimination of body waste products.

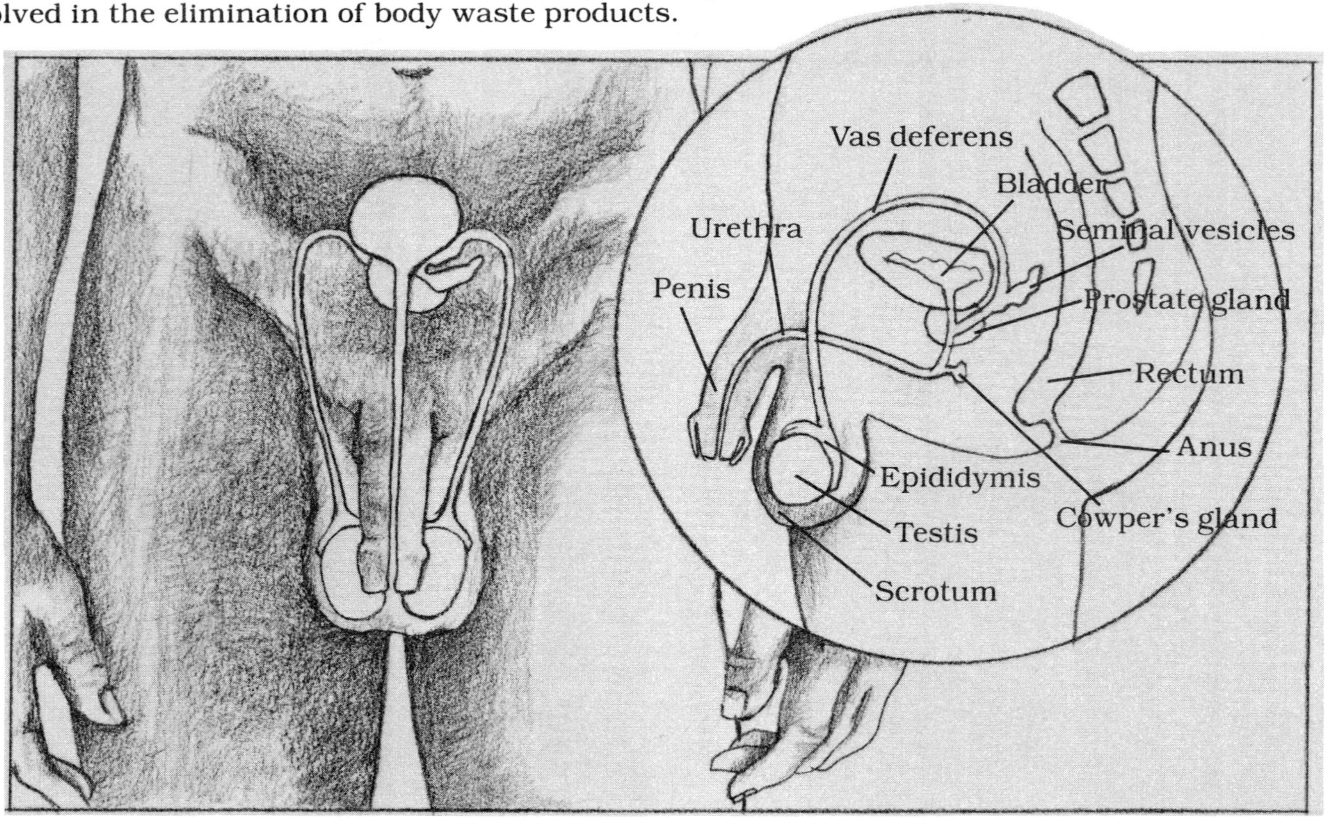

Vas deferens
Bladder
Seminal vesicles
Prostate gland
Rectum
Anus
Cowper's gland
Epididymis
Testis
Scrotum
Urethra
Penis

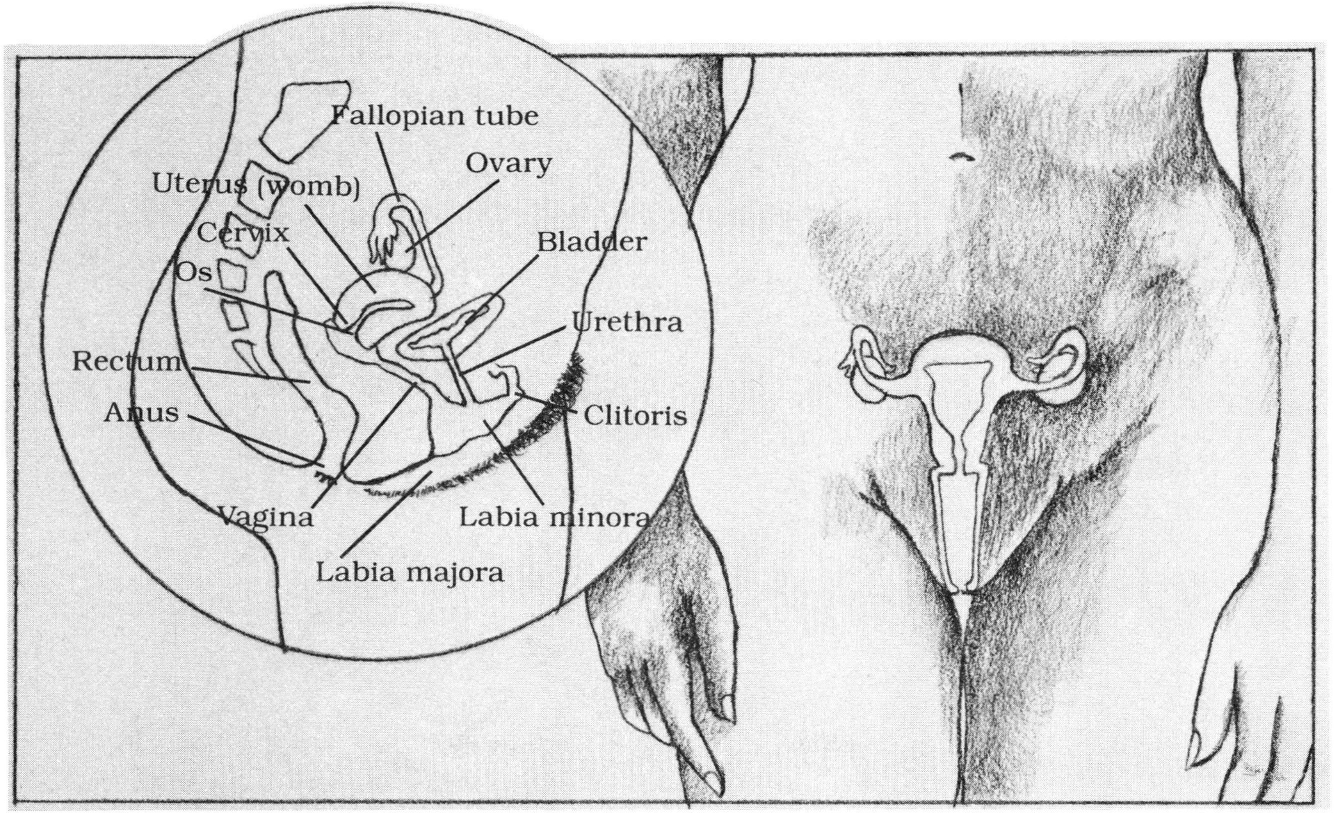

## Internal Female Genitals

These diagrams show side and front views of major parts of the female genital system, and nearby areas.

# The Process of Menstruation

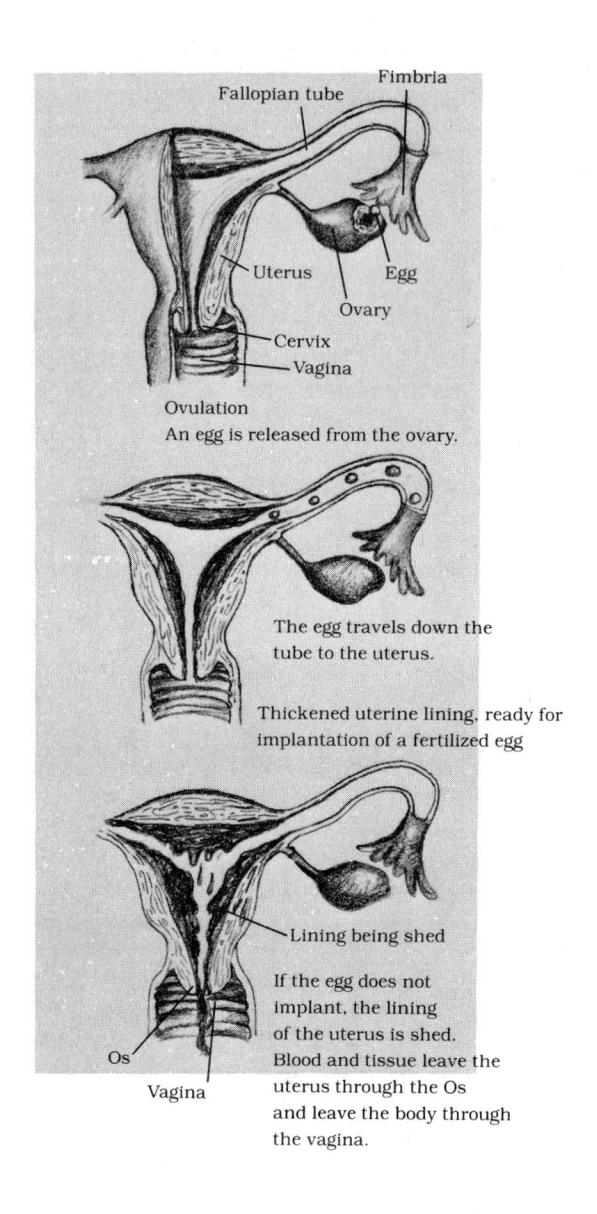

Ovulation
An egg is released from the ovary.

The egg travels down the tube to the uterus.

Thickened uterine lining, ready for implantation of a fertilized egg

Lining being shed

If the egg does not implant, the lining of the uterus is shed. Blood and tissue leave the uterus through the Os and leave the body through the vagina.

# Conception: How You Become Pregnant

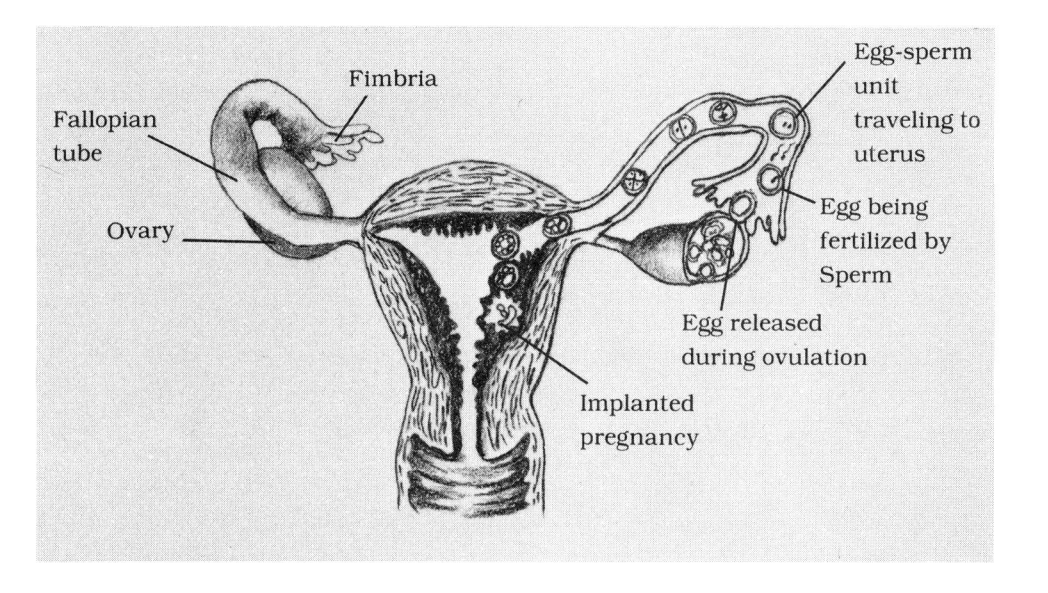

*Labels on diagram:* Fallopian tube, Fimbria, Ovary, Egg-sperm unit traveling to uterus, Egg being fertilized by Sperm, Egg released during ovulation, Implanted pregnancy

If you have had sexual intercourse with a man and used no birth control, if your birth control method hasn't worked, or if some semen from a man's penis has gotten close to the lips of your vagina and sperm have swum in, then the sperm will swim up the vagina through the cervical os into the uterus and then into the fallopian tube. The egg just released by the ovary may be penetrated by sperm. This can happen during two or three days a month. This is called *fertilization* or *conception*. Fertilization most often takes place in the fallopian tube. From there the fertilized egg takes about six days to move through the tube to the uterus, where it attaches itself to the inner uterine *wall*, or *lining*, and grows for about nine months.

While you are *pregnant*, hormonal signals sent to the uterine lining keep it thick and nourishing for the developing fetus. Because the lining is in use, you do not get your period. Not getting your period is one of the signs of pregnancy.

# Bibliography

Listed are some of the more practical works on parenting and on sexuality education in particular that you may want to read.

Bird, Joseph and Lois. *Power to the Parents,* Image Books

Buth, Lenore. *Sexuality: God's Precious Gift to Parents and Children,* Concordia Press, St. Louis, MO

Coleman, William. *Making TV Work for Your Family,* Bethany House Publishers, Minneapolis, MN

Curran, Dolores. *Who, Me Teach My Child Religion,* Mine Publications, Minneapolis, MN

Dodson, Fitzhugh. *How to Father,* New American Library, New York

Gardener, Ricahrd. *Understanding Children,* Jason Aronson, Inc., New York

Ginott, Haim. *Between Parent and Child,* Macmillan Publishing Co., New York

Gordon, Thomas. *Parent Effectiveness Training,* Peter Wyden, Inc., New York

Kenny, James and Mary. *Whole-Life Parenting,* Continuum Publishing Co., New York

Klien, Carole. *The Single Parent Experience,* Avon Books, New York

Satir, Virginia. *Peoplemaking: Because You Want to Be a Better Parent,* Science and Behavior Books, Palo Alto, CA

Thomas, David M., Editor. *Sex Education in the Family,* Abbey Press, St. Meinrad, IN